CHASING THE WIN

Becoming A Sales Leader

Ron MacKinnon

www.thewinprocess.com

National Library of Canada Cataloguing in Publication Data

MacKinnon, Ron, 1959-
  Chasing the win : becoming a sales leader / Ron
MacKinnon. -- Canadian bestseller ed.

ISBN 0-9731918-0-5

1. Selling. I. Title.
HF5438.25.M34 2003   658.8   C2003-910027-8

--

First Printing January 2003

Author: Ron MacKinnon
Formatting: Rick Dziadyk: Integration Marketing Works
Editor: Curtis G. Blair
Cover Design: Mike Schiebelbein: Integration Marketing Works
Illustrations: Integration Marketing Works
Printer: Friesens
Publisher: Montgomery Harrison Corporation:
                  Ron MacKinnon

Montgomery Harrison Corporation

         Phone: 403-819-6288
         Email: ron@thewinprocess.com
         Website: www.thewinprocess.com

         Printed and bound in Canada

To Sherri: my wife, mother of our children and my best friend.

I would never be in this position today if it wasn't for your faith in me. I love you and dedicate this book to you. Thanks for teaching me how to chase the win.

Contents

Section 1: Learning The Game 1

Section 2: Practicing The Game 87

Section 3: Winning The Game   193

Foreword

Ron MacKinnon is a Sales Leader.

But he was not born a Sales Leader. No one is. He worked at it. He studied numerous sales techniques. He learned from courses. He learned from his peers. He learned from his customers. He practiced what he learned. He demonstrated his abilities and became a Sales Leader.

The Win Process is the culmination of everything Ron has learned during his stellar sales career. But what makes Ron unique among his contemporaries is how this book is presented. This is not a *'how to'* book on selling. This is a *'how do'* book on becoming a Sales Leader. This book takes all you've learned about selling and answers the question -- how do I become and stay successful in sales?

Ron revisits many areas of the sales process and provides a fresh perspective. My favorite reflection in the book is a comment Ron makes to depict the typical decision making process. He notes that people buy from people they know and like. And in most industries, buyers view products and pricing as virtually indistinguishable between suppliers. So in the absence of a vendor-buyer relationship, selecting a vendor is like pulling a name from a hat.

Think about it. In most industries, the win ratio is 1:4. That means 75% of your opportunities, and the time and effort you put into them, are wasted. This fact alone is cause enough for you to read this book.

Chasing the Win is about developing the habits of a Sales Leader. It's about taking control of your sales career. It's not about theory. It's about application. It's not about having a funnel. It's about creating and managing a realistic, qualified funnel. It's not about being competitively priced in order to be in the game. It's about differentiating yourself with value in order to win the game.

How do you become and stay successful in sales? How do you become that which you aspire? How do you become unique? How do you gain control of your career, your future and your success? How do you increase your win ratio? How do you outsell, and not be outsold?

Become a Sales Leader.

- Curtis G. Blair

Acknowledgements

Writing this book has taken many hours of my time over the last six years but I certainly didn't write it alone. Throughout my life and career, there are a few people who had a major impact on my success today. These people deserve a special thank you.

Rose and Basil MacKinnon: My mom and dad taught me to be anyone I wanted to be. Thanks mom and thanks dad, you are always remembered and forever loved.

Rick Townsend: When we met, I was introduced to a new world of customer relationships. We started out as business associates and today we own a friendship that we both cherish. Thanks Rick, and may we get our 'hole in ones' on the same day.

Curtis Blair: Curt is an accomplished professional who fully understands all aspects of business. I am ecstatic he took on the task of editing my book. There were many changes and his meticulous effort is presented throughout these pages. Thanks Curt, it really looks great.

Rick Dziadyk: Rick is a dedicated entrepreneur and the most creative person I have ever met. His amazing capability in formatting and design is evident throughout this book. Thanks for bringing Elrude to life Rick. Your ideas will keep me going for years.

Montgomery John Cole and Harrison Jack Robert MacKinnon: My two boys are my life and every moment we are together we laugh and grow. Just when I thought there was no more to learn, my boys came along and took me by the hand. They have rounded me and made me whole. Thanks Cole and thanks Jack, I love you both.

Dave MacKinnon: I watched you turn your racing dream into a goal and win without ever giving up. You are my big brother and I learn from you. MacKinnon Racing Team forever.

Special appreciation

Tim Breithaupt for convincing me I am going in the right direction.
Les Hewitt for all his focused advice and motivating thoughts.
Andre Dagenais for showing me how to continually be successful.
Paul Gruhn for showing me how to be a polished presenter.
John Janzen for confirming my desire to succeed.
Mike Schiebelbein for his immense creative talent.
Frank Giancarlo for showing me in order to win you must go hard.
Sonny Vallieres for being my most valuable player in sales.

Introduction

Chasing the Win is about becoming a Sales Leader. It's about playing to win in the game of selling. If someone asked your boss or your peers or your customers if you are a Sales Leader, what would they say?

This book deals with the soft side of selling. It's about creating sales success by engaging the powers of knowledge, personality and desire. It's not about theory. It's about looking inward, and examining how we spend our time. It's about identifying and improving the areas we perceive we are not as strong as we should be.

I developed The Win Process® many years ago and I still use this approach today. It will work for you as well. The formula is simple. First we learn, then we practice and then we win. After all, isn't winning our goal?

The sales profession is the most misunderstood vocation in the world of work. It is not where you end up when there are no other jobs available. Being successful in sales takes hard work, commitment, integrity and intelligence. Selling is similar to most other professions in that there are skills you must learn and practice before you can be fully effective. Throughout this book you will learn about many of these sales skills and how they can help you become a Sales Leader.

This book is divided into three sections – Learning the Game, Practicing the Game and Winning the Game. In each section we discuss the selling attributes relative to that section, provide examples of how they are used, or in some cases – misused, and utilize cartoon characters and stories to demonstrate the points.

The language of selling may be universal, but there are still dialects specific to some industries. For example, there are many ways to refer to buyers – usually by the stage of the sales process. We call them suspects, prospects, customers, and clients, to name a few. But how we interact with buyers at any stage of the sales process remains constant. So in order to eliminate confusion, throughout this book I will use one word to identify buyers, regardless of the selling stage – customers.

Similarly, I use the word project to describe all types of sales opportunities – new business, cross selling, and up selling. We need to think of these activities as projects. They require a very focused mindset and encompass particular inputs in order to achieve the output we are looking for – a sale.

One other phrase I use is sales campaign. This describes our actual pursuit of business. Again, thinking of a prospective sale in this manner trains you to think in a logical, results-driven style. Becoming a Sales Leader requires careful preparation and attention to detail. There is very little room for winging it.

Let me introduce you to a couple of sales people who will illustrate the concepts of each chapter. Their exploits will make you think. They will test you and show you right from wrong. They will make you shake your head in disbelief and they will make you laugh. They will show you the difference between success and failure.

I believe there is a little bit of each of these characters in every one of us. Our challenge is to recognize which of their behaviors we exhibit and know where we need to improve.

Jack Coleman has been in the selling profession for 15 years. He has worked with four different companies in three different industries. All of his career changes were presented as opportunities to him because of his past success. He knows what it takes to win. He is a master strategist and completes his tasks in an efficient and timely manner.

Jack rarely loses a sales campaign. He is organized and his customers are his highest priority. He is a strong presenter and a good listener. He is in control of his sales efforts because he believes that is the only way to win. Most importantly, his customers all know him, trust him and love doing business with him. Jack Coleman is a Sales Leader.

Elrude Noclue has been in the sales profession for six years. During that time he has worked for five different companies in two separate industries. Unlike Jack, Elrude had no choice in his career moves. He has been fired four times.

Elrude doesn't understand his customers at all. He has never learned the skills of listening and understanding. But he certainly can talk, which quite often gets him into trouble. He is lazy and has limited or no relationships with his customers. He does not like to be in control because he believes that causes too much stress.

Elrude's victories are few and far between. Most of his customers have never heard of him and the ones who have don't trust him. Elrude's time at his current job is running out due to his lack of success. It will soon be time to move again. Elrude Noclue is not a Sales Leader.

Some sales people have asked me what would be the possible benefit to them from reading this book. After all, they tell me, they have a comfortable job, they are paid adequately, they have no hassles from their manager and their quotas are reachable with little effort.

The question I ask in return is what is your pay-off for being average? If you are not advancing your skills, you will soon be passed by those who are. What you do with your sales life is your choice. You can either be average or you can move forward and become a Sales Leader.

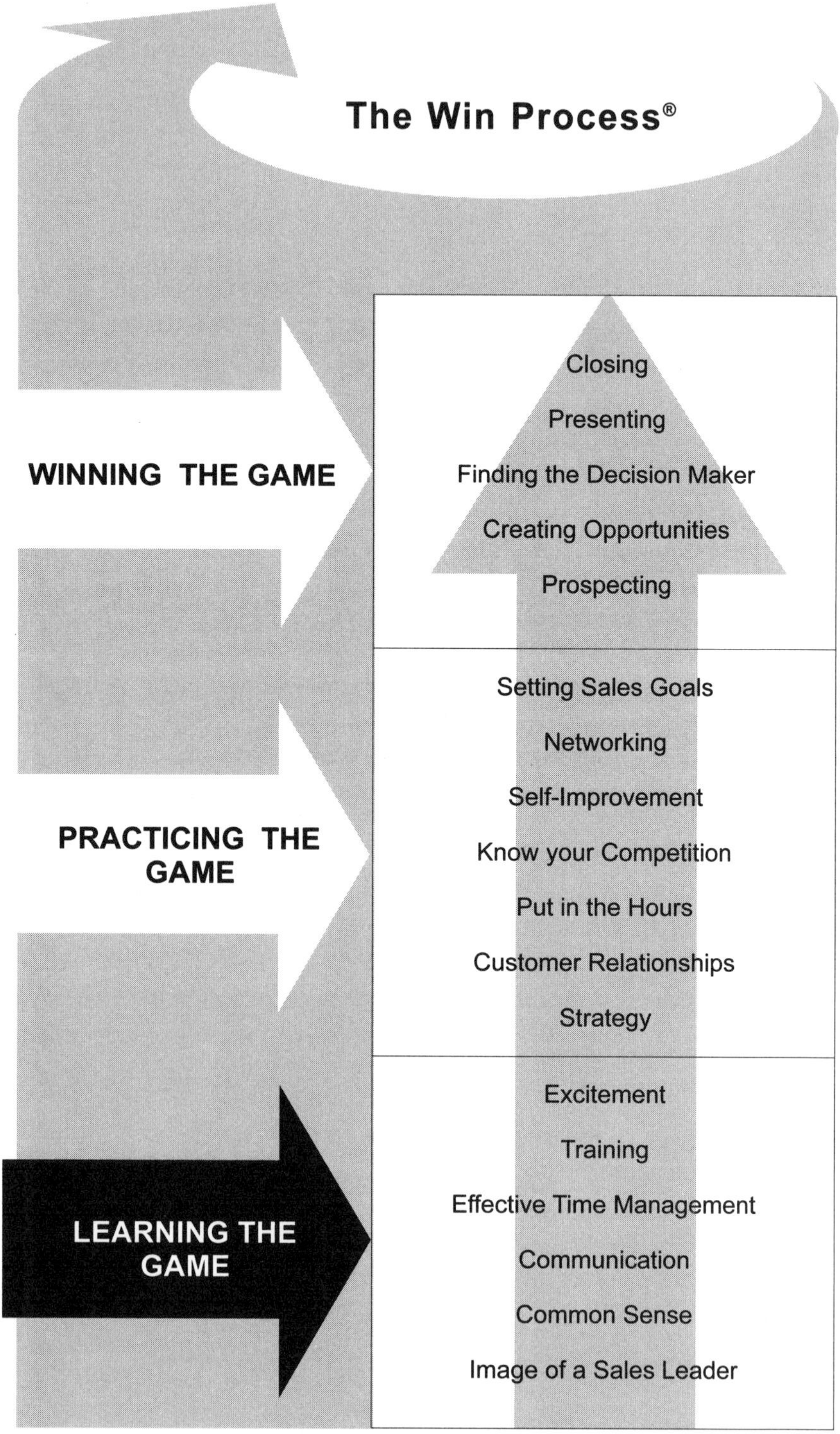

The Win Process®

WINNING THE GAME

Closing

Presenting

Finding the Decision Maker

Creating Opportunities

Prospecting

PRACTICING THE GAME

Setting Sales Goals

Networking

Self-Improvement

Know your Competition

Put in the Hours

Customer Relationships

Strategy

LEARNING THE GAME

Excitement

Training

Effective Time Management

Communication

Common Sense

Image of a Sales Leader

Section 1:
Learning the Game

Introduction

Before you can become a Sales Leader, you must adopt the behaviors of a Sales Leader. This first section of the book deals with understanding and developing the habits that will make you successful.

Mastering this section will be demonstrated by your ability to:

- Create and project the **Image of a Sales Leader**
- Use **Common Sense** in your daily activities
- Enhance your **Communication** skills
- Develop **Effective Time Management** practices
- Commit to continuous personal development through **Training**
- Generate **Excitement** in yourself, your co-workers and your customers

1 Image of a Sales Leader

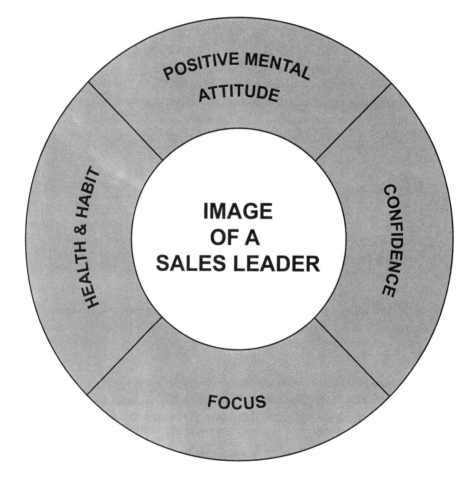

Image of a Sales Leader   1

First impressions have a lasting effect. During the initial seconds when meeting someone for the first time, you both size up each other and form an opinion – good, bad or indifferent. And that impression will stay with you until the other person proves you wrong or confirms your assessment. So what impression do your customers form of you? What image are you showing?

The image you portray comes from four sources – attitude, confidence, focus and your health and habit. It is important for you to know and understand these sources.

Every sales person has an image but few have the image of a Sales Leader. Your customers see what you are really like. They will decide very quickly if they like you or not. If they do not like your image, your chances of selling them anything will be slim. If they like your image, you will be on your way to building a successful relationship that will help pave a path for a successful career.

POSITIVE MENTAL ATTITUDE

What do your customers think about you when they meet you for the first time? Are they impressed? Are they uncomfortable? Are they excited? Are they turned off? Do you know how they really feel? Do you even care how they feel? Well you should if you want to become a Sales Leader. Take a moment to reflect on your attitude.

You must care about your customer's feelings. They make decisions based on their feelings. When your customers like you, the chances of doing business with them increase.

Win Tip
You get 5 minutes and that's all.

We are in total control of our attitude. We choose how we behave. And our behavior is influenced by our attitude. Replacing negative thoughts and feelings with positive ideas will help you in your business as well as your personal life. If you have a negative attitude when meeting with your customers, they will respond accordingly. Many sales people, although they don't realize it, exhibit a negative attitude.

Customers are on alert for negative attitudes from sales people. Many sales people will become defensive if the customer is not as eager to buy their product, as the sales person is to sell. Sales Leaders do not become defensive – ever. Your attitude must be sincere, helpful and respectful. Demonstrating a positive attitude will always put you in a good position throughout any sales campaign.

Stay positive. You will generate more success. Your day-to-day tasks will become easier to complete. And your ability to generate victories will surpass the goals you have set.

Win Tip
A positive attitude helps build trust.

A good way to stay positive is to control your actions. It's a great feeling to know what you have accomplished each day, and that you are one step closer to your goals. I've seen many sales people lose control of their actions, running from one customer to the next, wasting valuable time crisscrossing their territory. And at the end of the day, or week, or month, they are not sure what they have accomplished.

If this scenario describes you, stop this behavior now! Plan your approach. Develop a process that enables you to proactively visit all your customers, while allowing you to react to emergencies. When you plan your activities, you keep yourself occupied with meaningful work, always knowing what you will do next. Here's an example of a territory plan:

Step 1

- Build a list of all existing customers (include contact names, addresses, products/services purchased, competitors, future opportunities, etc.)
- Develop a contact strategy for each customer (weekly/monthly/quarterly, phone/personal visit, questions to ask, new information to share, etc.)

Step 2

- Build a list of all prospective customers in your territory (include all information you know and need to know about them)
- Develop a contact strategy for each business (weekly/monthly/quarterly, phone/personal visit, questions to ask, new information to share, etc.)

Step 3

- Plan your actions according to the contact strategy you have just developed. Some customers you will contact by phone monthly and visit quarterly. Customers can now be grouped geographically, so you won't be spending the majority of your time traveling. Of course the frequency and type of contact will change according to the needs of the customer, but you get the idea.

Your contact strategy should include keeping notes about all the information you uncover. There are many opportunities in your territory but they won't stand out for everyone to see.

Win Tip

If you do not show confidence when in front of your customer, do you think he will show confidence in you?

One of your roles is to displace your competitors, so make sure you know who your customers are buying from, their level of satisfaction, and what it will take to win that business. Now you can determine where you will spend your time and effort. This is where your positive attitude can help immensely by directing you to focus on the potential opportunities and not dwelling on the areas where you might not find any new business.

You now have a territory plan, a list of opportunities, competitive information and a contact strategy. Your chance of success has increased and you will feel better because you are winning, or at least moving in that direction.

You will be amazed at the time you save, the quality and quantity of your calls, and the satisfaction you receive knowing you are in control of your sales territory. This will provide a considerable boost to your attitude.

Win Tip

It's tough to be a winner without a positive attitude.

A positive attitude will enhance your selling abilities in two ways. First, when you show a positive attitude in front of your customers or co-workers, you generate an image of success and trust. People want to be around winners. A positive attitude is one of the most powerful sales tools that Sales Leaders use every day.

The second thing a positive attitude does is enable you to set and reach higher sales goals. With more sales comes more money for you. And isn't that one of the main reasons we're in this business?

ELRUDE

Jack Coleman has just spent the last two weeks learning all about a new product that could revolutionize the way some of his customers complete their day-to-day business. He has never sold a product like this before and has never met many of the decision makers in this area. Although he knows the product technically, he is not quite sure how to present it to his customer.

Jack knows that if he is excited about what this product can offer, his customer should be as well. He opens the meeting by asking a few questions to uncover possible applications for his new product.

Jack asks: How do you currently operate this portion of your business? How long have you been operating in this fashion? Would there be interest in upgrading/changing if new features were available that returned enhanced value for a small cost?

Elrude 1-1

Initially, the customer is not interested. Because Jack knows his product and how it can help this customer, he shares some success stories from similar businesses. Jack qualifies the opportunity and moves one step closer to a sale.

Jack's positive attitude guides him through the conversation. His customer is interested because he senses Jack's excitement and confidence. Jack uncovers a need and discusses his solution. His approach and his positive attitude gain his customer's trust.

Jack's approach and positive attitude enabled him to be successful. He could have very easily given up or became defensive when the customer said no the first time. Being positive, Jack knew if he positioned the solution properly he would be successful in moving to the next step. He did and he was. Constant positive thinking has become the backbone of Jack's selling strategy.

A positive attitude is like a breath of fresh air. Whatever you do or say has an impact on someone or something else. You have the ability to control whether that impact will be good or bad. A positive attitude helps. A negative attitude hinders. Think positive!

CONFIDENCE

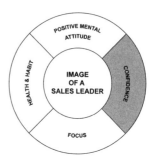

Confidence is how you feel about yourself, and how you project that feeling. Sales Leaders believe in who they are and what they have done. The way they walk and the way they discuss their success generates more opportunities for them. Customers want to deal with winners. When you demonstrate confidence in what you do, you actually make winning easier.

Hold your head high and be proud of yourself. How do you expect others to be proud of you if you are not proud of yourself? Some people tend to mope about, feeling that whatever they do, it will not work out for them. They don't want to take on anything new because they may not be good at doing whatever it is and they end up moping even more.

When I was a sales manager, I trusted my sales person who exuded confidence with an important task more then another sales person who moped around all day unsure of himself.

Let everyone know you are successful. People like to hear success stories – but don't overdo it. There are many ways to re-live these stories without bragging.

When you don't have confidence in your own abilities, how can you be successful? The answer is simple – you can't. People lack confidence because they are scared of making a mistake. How can you be confident doing something you have never tried before? Much of your self-confidence comes not from making mistakes, but from learning from your mistakes. You may lose a sale when you make a mistake, but you become more confident in your abilities to know you won't make the same mistake again. This is the confidence your customers need to see.

Win Tip

Confidence builds a winning attitude.

Confident people are winners. There are a lot of sales people out there who are not confident in themselves. None of them are Sales Leaders.

FOCUS

How many activities do you work on each day? How many of them do you accomplish? Sales Leaders are able to filter out distractions and focus on what needs to be done.

What some may think is a lot of extra work, these people routinely handle every day. They understand their customer's needs. They operate by the principal of ask, don't tell. They find out what their customer wants to buy and they sell it to her/him.

Wouldn't it be nice if we all could do that? Well we can. Selling is a simple process and many people make it tough by adding extra steps.

This is when we start losing sales and it boggles my mind the amount of times this happens. Why do we have to make things more complicated than they really are? I have thought about this for a long time and one day I came up with the answer.

I was playing squash one day with another person who was a better player than me. Our matches were the best three out of five and one day we were halfway through the third game when I came to realize the situation I was in. I had won the first two games fairly easily and was charging ahead in the third game until I started to lose my edge. At first, I thought it was because I was getting tired but before I knew it, the game was over and I had lost.

The more I tried to win, the worse I played. I kept getting into situations where I was playing catch up and running hard to stay in the rally. It was as if I had no control in the match at all. I kept thinking about what happened that changed the momentum from the first two games. Then it hit me. I had lost my control because I was trying too hard and I was adding extra shots into the rally that I didn't have to use. I became unfocused. When I was winning all I used were a few basic shots I could execute with total confidence. Feeling this was now too easy, I started to add some finesse shots that looked good. Problem was that I could not execute these shots as well therefore I was needlessly getting myself into trouble. When the match was over I had lost to this gentleman, but in the process I learned a valuable lesson.

Win Tip

When you are proactive and in control you demonstrate focus.

I learned I could beat my squash opponent with shots that were tight to the wall and hard for him to retrieve rather than trying to use the element of surprise.

The same holds true throughout a sales campaign. Always use your best tools and don't try new ones at a crucial point in the selling process. Practice new tools before you ever think of using them. Use the basics that got you there in the first place, no matter how boring these tools are. They are boring only because you have mastered them and you don't have to think how to use them. They just happen naturally for you.

Think back to when you were generating more success than you are today. Reflect on how you operated day-to-day when you were winning more often and compare that to how you are operating today. You may find slight differences that are contributing to your current struggles. Once you identify these differences, eliminate them and go back to operating the way you did when you were more successful. Use the tools that got you there in the first place.

Be Proactive

Another trait you need to be successful in this industry is being proactive. Sales people who are in control of their time are usually more proactive than others. And because they plan ahead, proactive sales people enjoy more success than others.

I mentioned earlier that if you prepare your next move, you are in control but if you don't prepare, then your competition gains the control. There are many good sales people who just can't seem to get on top of their day and they seem to fight this control all the time. All they have to do is stop for a moment and write out a plan. It doesn't need to be highly detailed, just the essence of what you must do to gain control of your activities. I will spend more time on this topic in Chapter Four.

When you have the ability to plan ahead, it also means you have the ability to change the plan if needed. When you find yourself in a situation where you don't feel comfortable with the direction the sales campaign is going, you can change the plan to keep yourself in control. Just imagine if you were not proactive and your competition had all the control. You would be able to see the end coming at you but not be able to do anything about it.

An easy example to think about for comparison is simply driving your car. Let's say your brakes have been squeaking for some time and you have not yet replaced them. One day while driving down a hill you realize that you have no brakes at all! You are now in a terrible situation and you have limited or no control. How would this feel compared to the other person who fixed those squeaky brakes and now has full control descending the same hill?

Push the Envelope

Pushing the envelope simply means to exercise your control with actions. Let's say, for example, that you have made it past the first few steps in the selling process and you have a solid relationship with your customer. This customer is getting ready to send out a quotation request to you and your competitors. You prefer this did not happen and you try to convince him to reconsider.

You provide proof that your pricing is competitive, technically you have the best solution, you offer the best after sale support, or any combination thereof. You must have a strong relationship in place with this customer in order to win with this tactic.

You are now pushing the envelope by going for the immediate win. You feel your chance for victory is better if you try to close the sale right now rather then play the game through to the end.

Essentially what you have done is put yourself in a much better position in the sales campaign. When you put yourself into a position where you can ask for the order – ask for it. Most people don't. Lever your control to move in for the victory when an opening presents itself.

HEALTH & HABIT

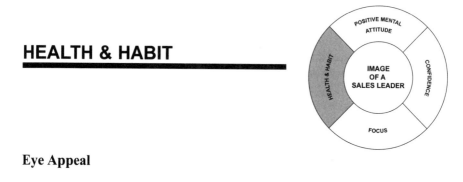

Eye Appeal

You must be pleasing to the customer's eyes by looking and acting professional. You might offer the best product, best price and best delivery but if you act and look like a slob, the sale could be jeopardized. Don't leave this to chance.

Sales people usually wear business attire. Some wear a suit while others are comfortable wearing a casual outfit. In either case, wear proper fitting clothes. I mentioned earlier that customers decide within the first few seconds of meeting you whether or not they are interested in doing business with you. If you don't put any effort into your choice of clothing and your appearance then you could lose before you even get started.

Jack Coleman and Elrude Noclue are competitors, trying to sell their product to the same customer. Both are attempting to see this customer for the first time. Although nobody knows this yet, Elrude's product is superior to and less expensive than the product Jack is selling.

Jack arrives for his appointment with this customer ten minutes early. He is dressed in a wool suit, cotton dress shirt and silk tie. He is wearing newly polished dress shoes. He doesn't sit until the customer offers him a chair. Jack controls the meeting by asking questions to understand exactly what the customer is looking for. He also offers information about how other organizations have used his product. Jack demonstrates he knows his product and has good ideas for its application with this customer.

Elrude 1-2

The customer is interested in what Jack has to say. He has already made up his mind that he likes this sales person and would like to do business with him. However, he is required by his company policy to look at another competitor.

Elrude shows up for his meeting ten minutes late and when he walks into the customer's office, the customer has an uneasy feeling. Elrude is wearing blue jeans with a too-tight dress shirt and a tie that is neither silk nor the proper length. His shoes have never been polished and his haircut has been out of style for at least ten years. At this point, the customer has made up his mind to not do business with Elrude.

The customer has just stack-ranked Jack far above Elrude, and even though Elrude's product is superior and lower-priced, he does not pay much attention to what Elrude is saying because he's focusing so much on what he does not like about Elrude.

Knowing that Elrude's price was lower, what would have happened if only

Elrude had taken the time to dress himself properly? He and his product more then likely would have stayed in the race. Winning a sale is a tough thing to do. One should not throw the chance away needlessly.

Dress professionally. Spend the extra money to buy quality clothes. When you look good, you feel good. When you feel good about yourself your confidence level rises; and confidence is a key element of success.

When you purchase clothing, put some effort into your decisions. First, wear clothing that is in style. There are variances to this depending on your personality, age and gender but use common sense in these decisions. A well-fitting wool suit should be your first purchase, followed by a cotton dress shirt. A silk tie is next and then socks and shoes. Black sneakers are not considered appropriate at any time. One very important rule to remember when you purchase clothing: Some colors and patterns should not be worn together. Clothing is very personal; I will leave it up to you to determine what looks best for you.

Win Tip

Black sneakers are not considered dress shoes at anytime.

Shoes are an important part of your wardrobe for a couple of reasons. First, is comfort – sales people spend a lot of time on their feet each day. If you wear inexpensive shoes your feet will quickly get tired, making the rest of your body tired as well. You need to be focused and awake.

Another reason why shoes are important is because shoes and socks complete your outfit. It makes me chuckle when I see sales people wearing a nice outfit but have elected to finish off their wardrobe with either black sneakers or white socks. (I am focusing on the male population of sales people because they need the most help. Women, for the most part, are simply better dressers. They don't seem to have the same issues as men when it comes to looking presentable in front of a customer.)

You should cover all the bases with your clothing. Going halfway just doesn't cut it. Oh, one more thing – shoe polish should be used regularly.

Healthy Lifestyle

Another way to look and feel good is to maintain a healthy lifestyle. This can be difficult to do because many sales jobs are not very kind to your health. For sales people who entertain clients in restaurants, the temptation to overeat or to eat the wrong food is overwhelming.

My suggestion is eat healthy foods like fruits, vegetables and proteins without all that sauce. Another way is to just eat light. You don't have to eat a large meal at lunchtime. Enjoy a hearty breakfast before you go to work and maybe a morning snack. When lunchtime arrives, you won't be as hungry for that large meal. Besides, heavy foods at lunchtime can make you tired in the afternoon.

Win Tip

Dress properly and take care of yourself.

Table manners can make or break a sale. Let's say you're the customer and two sales people were taking you out for lunch at the same time and one exercised perfect table manners while the other did not. Who would you feel more comfortable with? When we see someone chewing food while talking, we often choose not to look that way or talk with him or her. Don't let this happen to you. Learn and use proper etiquette and manners at all times when you are with customers or co-workers.

These may be small items to remember but they can put you in a favorable position with your customers. When you dress properly and take care of yourself, you increase your chances to make it to the next step of the sales campaign. Follow these ideas and you will be well on your way to a successful career and a happy lifestyle.

Summary

There are many important items that need to be addressed before you even hit the street in a sales campaign. You must design and maintain a positive mental attitude, for without one, you leave too much to chance. Dress properly and take care of yourself. The person your customer sees when you walk through the door will forever leave an imprint in their mind. You want that imprint to be in your favor.

Build as much confidence within yourself as you can. The more confident you are, the better you will feel when you are with your customers. This confidence will help you increase your sales almost immediately. Finally, your ability to filter out distractions and focus on what needs to be done will give you that extra edge over your competition.

In today's marketplace where the competition is greater than it has ever been in the past, something has to differentiate you from the competition. By implementing these tools of the Sales Leader, you will be more successful and you will be one step closer to catching the win you are continually chasing.

The **Image of a Sales Leader** will set the stage for your successful career in the sales profession. Before you do anything else, you must create a positive image. Fill this image with the following words and phrases that appear in this chapter and understand how each contributes to – or takes away from – the whole you.

Win Process:
Image of a Sales Leader

☑ Customers   Without one you will never have a sale

☑ Image   What others think of you

☑ Positive Attitude   Needed for victory

☑ Shoe Polish   Must cover every shoe you wear

☑ Healthy Lifestyle   Feel good about yourself

☑ Confidence   Know you are going to win

☑ Focus   Keep your eye on the ball

☑ Push the Envelope   You can make a difference

Win Notes: My Image

Use this page to assess your image. What are your strengths? Where do you need to improve?

2

Common Sense

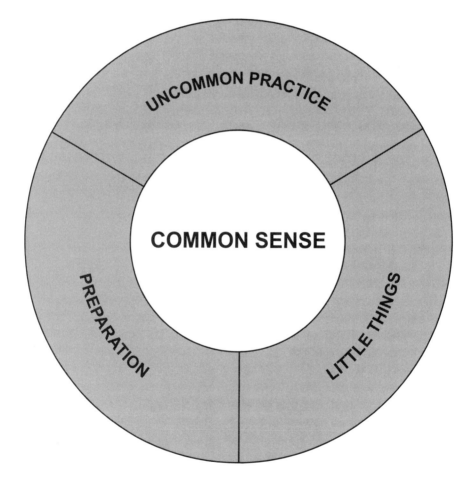

Common Sense

2

Half of every decision is derived from common sense yet most sales people never study this valuable tool. One of the most important concepts my father taught me as I was growing up was the ability to use common sense, and how it keeps everything in perspective.

So what is common sense? It is the message that is sent by the brain that helps people make the right decisions. When this message is released into action, it protects you from making ridiculous decisions like walking out in front of a moving vehicle, jumping from an airplane without a parachute or chasing a sale you are not going to win.

UNCOMMON PRACTICE

Here is an example taught to me by my father many years ago. When I obtained my drivers license, I was like most young kids starting to drive. Get your dad's car on the weekend and drive it as hard and fast as you could. Even in the small town where I grew up, this was dangerous, not only to me but also to my passengers and people in other vehicles.

My father taught me to drive sensibly and with care. He taught me to be aware of my surroundings when behind the wheel of a car. While other young kids were receiving speeding tickets, getting into accidents or just making other motorists miserable with their reckless driving, I used a different approach. I drove carefully and responsibly, earning credibility with the people living in my town. I didn't realize at the time that this was also a step in gaining credibility with the town-folk for future endeavors. What I did realize at the time was that I gained credibility with my friends who did not use common sense in their driving habits. I showed them I had patience and was careful while driving, so as to not endanger their lives. They appreciated this and usually asked to drive with me whenever we went somewhere.

When you use common sense in the sales profession, you move to a higher level of professionalism. There are not many people at this level so the competition is not as strong. Since that is the case then why aren't you on this higher level? Why don't you use common sense in your sales campaigns? Why don't you take advantage of a situation where the competition is limited? Why don't you move to the higher level of professionalism and bask in the success you deserve?

Win Tip

Common sense helps you make better decisions.

When you use common sense in your sales campaigns you will make better decisions, build better relationships, learn to be more patient, utilize effective preparation tools and gain a better understanding of your customer and their decision making style.

Many people who build customer relationships do an adequate job but sometimes that is not good enough to win the sale. You must get inside your customer's head and have a clear understanding of how he or she thinks. In most cases you will find there are many differences between you and your customers and it is up to you to make sure these differences do not have a negative effect on your sales campaign.

Win Tip

Common sense is an uncommon practice.

When something goes wrong between you and your customer, it does not mean your customer is at fault. It simply means you were not effective in presenting your point in a way that was meaningful to the customer. When you disagree with your customer, your relationship will not be affected if you use common sense. Disagreement does not mean dislike.

LITTLE THINGS

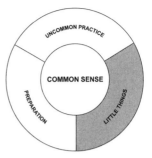

Let's look at a situation where a customer is trying to decide on a product to buy. This customer is in the market to purchase a new car. He has a small amount of cash and he also qualifies for financing. At one dealership a sales person tries to find the perfect car for this customer. The problems the customer cannot afford the kind of car he wants to purchase. The sales person tries to be creative by using the finance approach.

The sales person tells the customer that if he uses the cash he has as a down payment, he could finance the balance through a monthly lease. The customer agrees, they sign the deal and the customer drives away with a new car.

Two months later the customer wants to return the car because he can't afford it. The monthly payments are too high. The sales person will not return the money and cancel the transaction, but offers to trade the car in on another vehicle.

There are a number of questions that arise from this situation:

- Did the customer use common sense when he purchased the car?
- Did the sales person use common sense when he sold the car?
- Did the sales person use common sense when the customer came back to return the car?

The answer to all these questions is no.

Let me explain why. The customer made an emotional decision to purchase the car and simply threw all logic out the window. When he entered the dealership the customer knew he had choices – buy a car he could afford and pay cash, or lease a more expensive one, but not both. He put himself too far in debt when he said yes to the deal he signed. If he had used common sense, he would have stayed within his budget even if it meant expanding his search or delaying his purchase.

The sales person, on the other hand, should not have sold that car to the customer. He knew his customer could not afford to give away all his cash and take on a monthly lease as well. By not using common sense the sales person now has an unhappy customer. For the sales person it came down to a battle of common sense against greed, and greed won out. He too could have demonstrated patience and creativity by utilizing common sense.

Win Tip

Common sense is the ability to complete all the little things right without thinking about them.

When the customer came back to return the car, the sales person had another opportunity to make this customer happy but by refusing the customer's request he made the situation worse. He should have discussed options with the customer (sell the car, rewrite the lease over a longer term, etc.) and won back a happy customer. He had a second chance but he failed again to use common sense.

The result now is the very unhappy customer has a car he can't afford. He will likely never go back to that dealership again. And we all know that unhappy customers talk more about their bad experiences then happy customers talk about their good experiences. This sales person has earned a reputation he would rather not have. And if he does not start using common sense, his sales, not to mention his career, will suffer. The dealership and the leasing company lose as well because in the mind of the customer, they allowed this situation to happen.

This could have been avoided if all parties used common sense. The sales person knew in his heart that the customer could not afford that car but he was greedy and put pressure on the customer anyway. His short-term thinking lacked common sense, getting him nowhere in the sales field.

Had the sales person and the leasing agent acted in the best interest of the customer, they may have waited longer to get the deal, but they would have gained a happy customer and a reputation for excellent service. And, as you'll read further in the book, building relationships based on mutual trust plays an important part in becoming a Sales Leader.

You can see by this example that decision making requires common sense, and when well executed, provides an excellent return on investment.

PREPARATION

Common sense is never more important than during the preparation stage of your sales campaign. Why do some sales people prepare every move while others just seem to float along?

The answer to that question is simple. The people who prepare are using common sense. What else could it be? We discussed in the previous chapter that if you prepare your moves in the campaign, you will have a higher chance of victory while others who don't prepare usually fall behind.

People who think they will win sales campaigns without putting in the effort to organize and prepare are only fooling themselves. Preparation can be the primary reason why you win a sale. So by using common sense to help you prepare, you are putting yourself in a better position.

ELRUDE

Elrude Noclue and Jack Coleman have both recently completed presentations for the same customers. Although the content of Jack's presentation was better then Elrude's, no decision had yet been made.

Both sales people were left to sweat it out for almost a week before the final decision was announced. Jack Coleman was victorious while Elrude would be forced to move on and try again another day. The customers believed that both solutions would work for them and the prices were very close as well.

The final decision came down to the presentation. The ultimate decision maker within the group of customers became uneasy with Elrude because he would never make eye contact with him. When Elrude delivered his presentation, he unknowingly picked one individual out of the group and continued to look at him while presenting.

Elrude 2-1

Elrude was also in a position where he did not know the answers to all the questions that he was asked. Normally not a problem, however he never wrote the questions down so he could remember to answer them later. The customers' perception is that Elrude would forget to respond with the answers.

Let's look at the Elrude example. Small parts of Elrude's presentation became the glaring issues that lost him the sale. Common sense eliminates these types of events from happening if you just take the time to think. Jack used common sense because he was aware he needed to address all participants equally in the boardroom during his presentation. He realized that if a person was taking the time to attend his presentation, there was a good chance they were involved in the decision making process as well. Elrude just assumed that would happen naturally and never gave it any thought.

Win Tip

Preparation is common sense.

Summary

Common sense is one of the most important tools you will ever use in a sales campaign. It will help make better decisions and gain a better understanding of your customer. Common Sense is very uncommon. Let's make it common in your life and help you win more sales.

Common Sense is an uncommon practice in the world of selling. When you use common sense as part of your overall selling strategy you will become an uncommon Sales Leader. Integrate common sense into your overall strategy with the help of these following words included in this chapter and understand the actions.

Win Process:
Common Sense

☑ Perspective   Insight to the selling world

☑ Right Decision   Think before you make one

☑ Credibility   Your customer's view of you

☑ Analytical   Ability to think

☑ Little Things   Pieces to help you win

☑ Patient   Waiting for the right time

☑ Uncommon Practice   Execution of common sense

☑ Preparation   Getting ready for battle

Win Notes: My Common Sense

Use this page to assess how you use common sense. What are your strengths? Where do you need to improve?

3 Communication

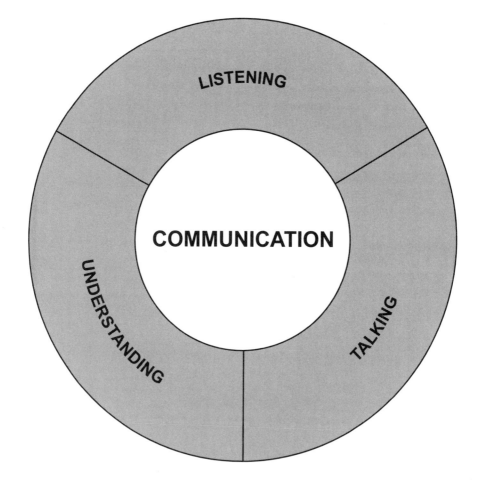

Communication 3

How do you become a Sales Leader? By talking faster, louder and longer then your competition? Let me tell you that if you believe this is the path to sales greatness you must stop talking and listen.

While you are out there talking faster, louder and longer to your customers, your competition is stealing your business. Communication is one of the best tools you can ever use in a sales campaign. Without it you will never know what your customer wants to buy.

Miscommunication is one of life's largest problem areas. It causes many headaches, heartaches, disappointments and wrong impressions. Here is an example of how that can happen and unfortunately does to many sales people.

Win Tip

Stop talking faster, louder and longer and you will be more successful in sales.

At the start of the year a sales person asks his manager for details about a bonus plan for the upcoming year. The manager has yet to put together all the details of the plan but he has a few ideas about what he would like to see.

Instead of telling his sales person the plan is not finalized yet and he should check back in a few weeks, he starts telling him about his ideas. The sales person doesn't realize these are just ideas. He believes what he is hearing is the actual plan.

He becomes quite excited about his future possibilities and spends the rest of the year working very hard to exceed his quota.

When the year is over, the sales person believes he will make an additional sum of money based on his conversation at the start of the year. Unfortunately, his manager has forgotten everything he told this sales person and there is no bonus plan in place at all.

There will be fireworks over this one and when the smoke has cleared, the sales person will most likely further his career with another company.

Similarly, imagine if your customer wanted to buy the blue round object but you wanted to sell him the red square object because you never took the time to ask him which one he wanted. Are you going to win that sale?

Communication is made up of three parts: listening, understanding and talking. Sales Leaders excel in all these areas.

LISTENING

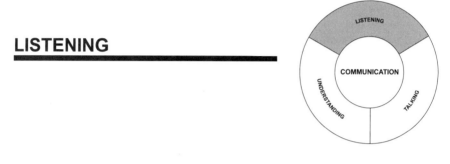

If sales people would only listen properly they would increase their sales success almost immediately. Why is listening so important?

We need to listen in order to understand what our customers want to buy. But how do we listen? Do we just walk into their office, sit down and say nothing?

Proper listening requires preparation. Ask high gain questions and pay attention to the answers. Never tell your customers what they want to buy. This usually does not go over very well. Discover your customer's needs and wants by asking both open and closed questions. Ask your customer why they need to purchase this new product and let them explain their reasons. Ask them when they need this product and let them tell you their time frame. Ask them exactly what it is they need and let them tell you in detail. Ask them who will be involved in the final decision of the purchase and let them give you names of other individuals involved. Ask them where the product or service will be used and where the decision will be made. Finally, ask them what their decision making criteria are for this sale. An

Win Tip

Listen to what your customer wants and give yourself the order.

example is if they are buying based on lowest price instead of higher quality. You need to understand these criteria so you don't sell higher quality instead of lower price.

When you ask high gain questions you are in fact communicating at a high level. Once you have completed your meeting you will know most of the criteria involved so you can provide a targeted solution response for your customer. All you did was begin your discovery by asking basic questions and let your customer provide the answers. You talked for a minimal amount of time and your customer talked the majority of the time. Two interesting actions have now just happened. You gained quite a bit of data that you can use to advance to the next step in the sales cycle. And you left a good impression on your customer because you listened to his wants and needs.

Win Tip

How do you expect to sell your customers anything if you don't let them tell you what they want?

Listening is the most important element of communication. Many people think in order to communicate you must talk to someone. You have to tell them things. This is just not true.

Let's talk about divorce, a common event caused, in many cases, by ineffective communication. Some marriages break up because one person builds up a series of issues but does not communicate them to the other person. Then one day the issues have grown so large that the person just walks away from this life-long commitment.

If something as valuable as a marriage can be destroyed by lack of communication, then sales campaigns, which are not nearly as important, can be decimated as well. I have seen many situations where a sales person had the right solution for the sale; the best price and delivery but still lost the deal. Communication paths between the sales person and the customer were simply ineffective. These sales people continued to talk and talk. The customer became annoyed and bought the product from someone else.

I am sure you have heard the saying silence is golden. Well, it truly is golden in the sales world. One of your best attributes is to know when to speak and when to listen.

TALKING

Believe it or not, there are times when sales people must talk. Most communication is bi-directional, but talking in a sales campaign should be kept to a minimum when it comes from the sales person. You want your customer to do most of the talking.

I mentioned earlier that you must ask high gain questions in order to get the answers you require. Then you let your customer answer these questions with valuable information that you will need to win the sale. The more high gain questions you ask, the more high value information you will receive.

Direct your customer to tell you exactly what they need, why they need it, when they need it and how much they want to pay for it. Ask who will make the final decision in their company to buy it. (Be careful and thorough with this because information gatherers will quite often tell you they are the decision maker.) You are moving yourself closer to obtaining the order by gaining the information you need. You are in fact awarding this order to yourself and your company. This is called total control and you get it by talking at the right time and for the right amount of time. Some questions you could ask are:

- What exactly are you looking for?
- What color does it need to be?
- What size do you need?
- Why do you need this?
- Are there any other ways to achieve the same results?
- What is your timeframe for purchasing this?
- Is this when you want it or when you plan to order it?
- Are you OK with a four week delivery?

- What is your budget for this purchase?
- How much do you expect to actually pay for this item?
- How do you expect to pay for this item? (Purchase order, lease, net 30, etc.)
- Who will make the final decision?
- Is there anyone who can veto the decision?
- So, you are the final decision maker, am I correct?

Have you ever noticed that the best sales people will usually say price is almost never an issue, while less successful sales people continue to ask for discounts? Sales Leaders have learned that total control means you are putting your customer in a position where they do the talking and you do the listening. A lot of sales are won or lost right here while communicating with your customer.

Sales people will get an opportunity to talk. There is usually a time in the sales campaign where you tell your customer what you are going to sell them. We call this the presentation stage and I will cover it in more depth in a later chapter, but let's take a moment to look at the philosophy now.

By listening first, you will obtain all the information you need to present the exact product or service your customer wants to buy. You are in fact presenting the solution they want to hear. Your competition may have a similar product but they might not have taken the time to ask what the customer wanted. The presentations for your customer will unfold like this: You present a solution based on what your customer needs. You are actually giving back to them exactly what they told you they needed. You are presenting it to them simply by showing what they asked to see.

If your competition is not listening to the customer, then chances are they are doing most of the talking – and telling your customer about their product. They are not presenting a solution. Your competition will lose because they never took the time to listen earlier in the sales campaign. All they did was talk. They talked at the wrong time and for the wrong amount of time. Now their chance of giving the customer what he or she really wants is quite low. They don't know what the customer wants because they did not ask nor did they listen. You will probably walk away with the victory.

UNDERSTANDING

This is the part of the sales campaign that ties communication in a nice little bow. Throughout the listening stage you absorbed all the useful information about what your customer needs to buy. Then you presented your product to him or her in a manner whereby you gave them a solution to their problem. All this would not be possible if you did not understand why or how your solution fit the customers' need.

Throughout both the listening stage and the talking stage you must fully understand all issues and reasons. You do this by asking for clarification. If you do not understand something your customer said, then ask him to clarify it for you. Clarity is the key to strong and effective communication. Never be embarrassed to say you don't understand something your customer says.

You must understand your customers' reasons for wanting or needing a certain product or service. When you understand him or her then it is easy to provide a solution. When you don't understand what he or she needs then it becomes a guessing game and you don't want to put yourself in that position. Make the effort to understand what is needed and why it is needed so you can later present the solution he or she desires.

Let's review this wonderful tool called communication. First you ask and listen then you provide answers by talking and at the same time you understand:

■ Exactly why the customer needs the product or service,
■ How it will be used,
■ When it is required,
■ Who will be using it and will benefit from it
■ Where it will be delivered or applied

■ What all the decision-making criteria are and who is involved.

Just think, if your competitors don't have this information, their proposals will be product-out, while yours will be customer-in. Now, who is the customer more likely to buy from?

ELRUDE

Jack Coleman has just been awarded a sale he has been chasing for 18 months. In his post-victory debrief with his customer, he was told that he delivered exactly what his customer wanted. He also delivered the solution within budget.

Elrude 3-1

Throughout the entire sales campaign, Jack asked questions and took note of all the answers. He allowed his customer to do most of the talking while he listened. Jack listened until he was convinced he understood all the details of what his customer wanted. If there was something he did not understand, he asked more questions and allowed his customer to answer them. This process went on until Jack was convinced he knew exactly what his customer wanted, when it was needed and what the price had to be. He then delivered what his customer wanted.

Elrude Noclue was at the wrong end of the stick again. He couldn't believe he lost this one. He thought he knew exactly what his customer was looking for. During that first meeting, Elrude knew right away where his customer was going when he asked about a specific feature.

When Elrude delivered his presentation a few weeks later he felt he had momentum and thought his presentation was strong and to the point. He laid everything out for the customer. He told him exactly what he needed.

During his debriefing session he was amazed to find out his price was too high, his delivery was off by almost two months and the actual product he presented was not what the customer really wanted. If only he had known earlier in the selling campaign, he could have done something about it.

I once heard about a sales person who won a large sales campaign and he was involved in the sales process for less then three days. His competition had been chasing this project for almost two years.

'John' was competing with four others on an international project. There are many steps to the sales campaign, as we all know, but in this particular case John was starting his sales campaign far too late. That didn't help his chances so he had to put some thought into his approach. He knew his competition well. He also knew that clarity was the key to effective communication. John asked for only one favor – he wanted to be the last sales person to present his solution.

John never got the chance to find out all the information he needed for an effective presentation and he did not want to perform a standard product demo.

He had half a day to conduct a full presentation on the product he was offering to his customer. When his customer and associates walked into John's boardroom they were almost sure they were not going to buy his product. John started his presentation by asking his customer what he wanted that has not yet been provided by any of his competition. After a moment or two of silence his customer mentioned a few items that he would like to see which were not provided. John had a starting point. He then asked why these features were important and again his customer provided him with answers.

John now had something unique to show his customer that none of his competition had shown. He knew his competitions' product was similar to his but he wasn't about to tell his customer that. As a matter of fact, he paused for only a moment and in his mind he thanked all his competition for this opportunity. By not communicating properly with the customer, all of the competitors merely presented their product and missed valuable information. John moved into total control and knew he was going to win this sale.

John spent the next hour showing his customer exactly what he wanted to see. Within this hour John uncovered several more needed features that his competition neglected to show.

John continued with this approach until there were only fifteen minutes left in the presentation. Almost four hours had passed since the presentation started and John asked many tough questions. Through these questions he was able to motivate his customer to talk in great detail about himself, his company, his fellow workers and this new product he was about to buy.

John concluded by explaining he could offer everything his competition offered plus all these other features and benefits they didn't offer, and for a similar price. He asked his customer if there was anything else he needed and the reply was no. His customer was very pleased with John's solution. Three days later John was awarded the order.

John's solution was no better or worse than any of his competitor's. He won because he presented the right benefits. He presented the right benefits because he took the time to listen to what his customer was asking for. He out-smarted his competition and took advantage of the opportunities they gave him.

It took John four hours to gain total control and win while it took his competition almost two years to lose. He won because he communicated better than all his competition.

I am not suggesting that you treat each and every potential victory like this. What I am saying is that even in grave circumstances you can still win. When you have the most information you are quite often in a better position for the victory. Sometimes you can obtain this information rather quickly.

Summary

Communication is listening first than talking, after you understand what your customer needs. It doesn't matter how long this valuable sales step takes to complete as long as it is completed with clarity.

Communication becomes one of your most important tools in winning the sales you chase. Understanding the wants and needs of your customer puts you in a unique position to deliver those goods. Listening intently to your customer allows you to obtain the information you need to proceed with your sales campaign.

Win Process: Communication

☑ Talking   Let your customer do it

☑ Listening   You do it

☑ Understand   Make sure you do

☑ Clarity   So everyone understands

☑ Information   The fuel you need to win

☑ Bi-directional   Both directions

☑ Increase Sales   Derives from listening and understanding

☑ Questions   Ask as many as you can

Win Notes: My Communication

Use this page to assess your listening, talking and understanding skills. What are your strengths? Where do you need to improve?

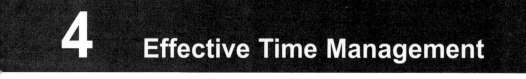

4 Effective Time Management

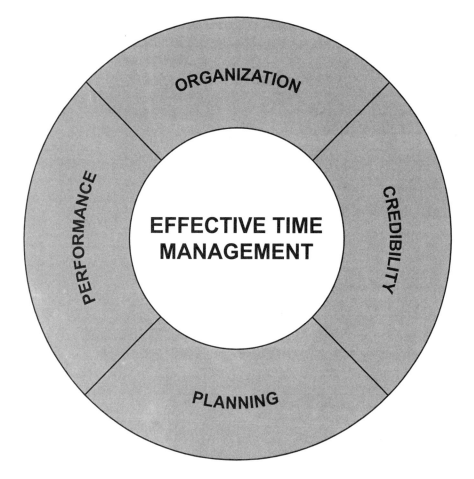

Effective Time Management   4

Effective time management can make the difference between an average sales person and a Sales Leader. If you don't control your time and what you are doing with it then you are probably wasting it. And time is the one thing you cannot save for later use.

Sales Leaders use effective time management in all their activities because it helps them win more sales. There are four parts to effective time management that you must understand and master: Organization, Credibility, Planning and Performance.

ORGANIZATION

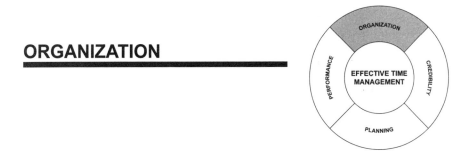

Workspace

The first step to becoming organized – is cleaning up your desk space. We have enough distractions from our co-workers, email and phone calls. A cluttered desk just adds to the confusion. Start by taking everything off your desk except your telephone. Now you can dedicate parts of your desk to certain job functions.

First, pick the area on your desk where you plan to complete all your writing. This now becomes sacred for that task only. Do not use this space for anything else. It is not for placing papers on or setting books on or your briefcase or purse. It is used for when you are writing – period!

Next, select the area on your desk where you plan to keep your active paperwork. This is usually paperwork or files that need attention on a regular basis. For example, documents related to a sale you are currently chasing and the customer is calling you often to ask questions and obtain information.

Never file documents permanently on your desk. That is what a file storage system is for. Adopt the rule that if you are not currently working on it, then file it. When you have too many files on your desk you could spend all your time moving from file to file without actually getting anything completed. Worse than this, you could have a file buried under another file and when you find it again, it is too late to do anything with it. You may have even lost a sale.

People who do not clear a working area on their desk tend to miss or misplace important pieces of information. When you deal with many different customers and with many different projects you must be organized or you can become overwhelmed.

Your work area needs to be free from documents and paper and books and whatever else might accumulate there. Should you have too much paper on your desk, you will work only on what is on top of the pile. If someone puts information on your desk while you are working on another file, in most cases you will stop what you are doing and start working on whatever was just placed on your desk. This is called working from the top down. It is very ineffective. Never put yourself in this position.

A better design is the task method. Here you plan your day according to your priorities. Identify what needs to get done, and how much time you will allow. Occasionally – or frequently for some of us – emergencies or interruptions can throw our plans into chaos. To account for this, book time between tasks to review email, consult with others or handle unexpected tasks. You will find this method causes less stress, less desk clutter, and leaves you feeling good about what you have accomplished.

Use your desk for what it was designed for and you will become more effective and organized at managing your work. This, in turn, will make you more successful because you will be able to accomplish tasks faster and with better quality.

File Storage

When you organize your desk properly you will likely find a large pile of documents and paperwork has piled up and you must put it somewhere. You will need a filing drawer or a filing cabinet. Take a moment to decide how you want to set up your files.

Usually files are arranged in alphabetical order, but other methods are used as well. For example, sales documents could all be filed under one heading while customer files could be filed under another heading. Whichever way you choose, make sure your system is consistent. This is especially important if other people in your office have access to your files. If you are away from your desk and they have access to, and understand your filing system, they can help with customer inquiries. This is a level of service that only Sales Leaders provide, and customers appreciate it.

These files are now out of your way and you take them out as you need them. Don't forget to put them back after you have finished using them. Doing this keeps your working area clean and free from paper junk.

Once you have these files set up you now have a place to store all the documents or paperwork pertaining to that topic or customer. By having all that information in one place it becomes a lot easier to control.

Scheduling Calendar

An important tool in your sales life is a scheduling calendar. There are two different types available – paper or plastic. Decide which style is best suited for you. Personally, I favor the electronic (plastic) type. Mine can store thousands of contact names, addresses, phone numbers, cell numbers, email addresses, to-do lists, notes – the list is endless. Sales people who use a calendar properly are more organized and successful than those who don't use one properly or at all. It is almost impossible for anyone to remember everything they need to do, when they need to do it, who they need to do it with, where they need to do it, which customer they need to do it for... You get the picture.

Win Tip

Unless you can remember everything, you need a scheduling calendar.

Many electronic schedulers can link to and exchange files with your computer email program. The feature alone is worth the price of the handheld unit. If you don't have one, get one. Consider it an investment in yourself.

ELRUDE

Elrude Noclue has just started work with a new company. He has taken over from another sales person who has been promoted. Elrude inherits a large number of accounts. One of his new customers is involved in a new project and needs to buy equipment.

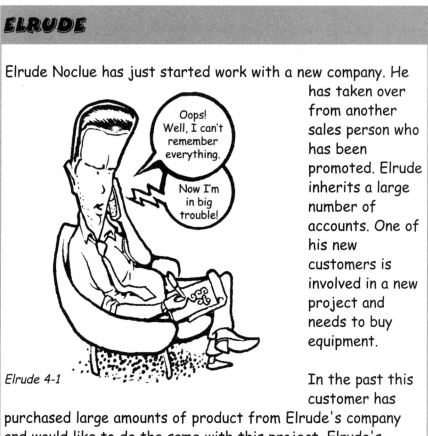

Elrude 4-1

In the past this customer has purchased large amounts of product from Elrude's company and would like to do the same with this project. Elrude's predecessor was organized. For several years he provided his customer with a high level of support. The customer expected the same level of service from Elrude.

When the account change took place, Elrude was told what he had to do in order to keep this customer happy. Elrude agreed that it would be best to provide the same sales support that his predecessor provided.

Elrude struggled with this account, adding days and sometimes weeks to the delivery time because he never properly completed the paperwork before submitting his orders. Therefore the people in the manufacturing department were not quite sure what Elrude wanted for his customer. They had to ask for clarification and this added time to the delivery process. Elrude placed four orders for this customer and all these orders were late. On two of the orders, wrong equipment was ordered and delivered.

Elrude never wrote down any questions the customer asked him and promptly forgot about them as soon as he left his customer's office. His customer expected answers the next day but never received them. He would call Elrude two or three times just to get a simple answer.

These questions were usually not very hard to answer, however Elrude was not familiar with his company's products and had to look up the answers in his product books.

This frustrated the customer, causing him to call someone else in Elrude's company and receive an answer immediately. Elrude always had an excuse about being too busy or he couldn't find the answer. One day his customer decided that enough was enough.

Elrude tried his best to support the customer but constantly ran into problem after problem. He also found that this one customer was taking up most of his time, keeping him from regularly calling on his other accounts.

One day Elrude's manager called him into his office and told Elrude he was taking this account away from him. Elrude couldn't believe it. He had no idea the customer was unhappy. And he was shocked to hear this from his manager. Whenever this happened before the customer would tell Elrude he was unhappy, and together they worked to resolve the issue.

Unfortunately, this time the customer had already made up his mind that he did not want to deal with Elrude any longer. As a matter of fact, he told Elrude's manager that he would take his business elsewhere if a change was not made immediately. Elrude lost this account without any discussion.

The reason for the quick decision was obvious. Elrude's manager did not want to lose one of his largest accounts. Elrude had the account taken away from him because he was disorganized. The customer was accustomed to getting his product on time and his questions answered promptly.

The sales person who took over the account from Elrude is very organized and the customer quickly became happy again. He receives his orders without delay and he gets all his questions answered in a timely fashion.

Considering it takes many times the sales and marketing costs, time and effort to land a new customer then it does to retain an existing one, the answer is simple. You must be organized if you want to be successful in sales. Your customers will demand it, your competition will provide it and your results will reflect it.

Whenever you take over an existing customer base, you need to get your arms around it as quickly as possible:

- Meet with the former rep and review the complete customer list in detail (Contact names, files, outstanding issues, pending orders, etc.)
- Visit each customer with the outgoing rep to ensure a smooth handoff and transition.

Understand the current customer/sales person relationships and look for ways to duplicate or improve them.

CREDIBILITY

A key element that comes from effective time management is credibility. We talked about organization skills and the problems that can be caused from not using this important sales tool. Now let's look at how it affects your credibility.

Most people like to be trustworthy and credible, and sales people are no exception. Sales people thrive on being told they are credible and trustworthy – especially when the customers are saying it! We all know the generic stigma associated with sales people. Sales Leaders do not fit that mold. In fact, Sales Leaders go out of their way to not fit that stereotype.

Let's go back to Elrude. After all is said and done, how does Elrude's customer feel about him as an individual? He may like Elrude as a person but because he has lost trust in him as a reliable sales person, problems occurred and the relationship suffered. What happens if this customer is asked by another customer to provide a reference for Elrude and his company?

If the new customer finds out that Elrude has been unreliable or held no trust from his past customer, then the potential sale could be in jeopardy. We don't want that to happen to us.

As a customer or as a sales manager, how would you feel if you suddenly found out your sales person could not be trusted? What if you found out that your sales person had no interest in answering questions? What would you think if you discovered your sales person could not get orders entered on time, causing unnecessary delays?

Effective Time Management

Sales Leaders recognize the importance of effective time management, and have developed the proper habits to ensure they get their work done as quickly as possible. One habit you should develop when in front of your customer is take notes. Whatever questions they ask you, write down so you don't forget them.

Even today with the advancements in technology that allow us to use a variety of electronic organizers, we still need paper and pen. It remains the easiest and quickest way to keep accurate notes. Sure it feels great and represents status to us to be able to type meeting notes onto a small touch-screen apparatus using a stylus. It makes us feel even better to know that when we return to our office, we can download the data to our computer.

It's all very exciting; however, in the end we still need a piece of paper for our file with information on it. The only importance about that piece of information is its accuracy. It doesn't really matter how the information got there. I am a strong proponent of electronic organizers and high-speed computers. I own both and use them regularly but I still use a pen and paper when I am taking notes, no matter where I am.

Win Tip

Write it down.

Write it down.

Write it down.

Customers are ordinary people and they know how hard it is to remember things. They are not fooled for a minute when you say you will remember what they asked. You are not the only sales person who calls on this customer and you are not the only one who doesn't write their questions down. Therefore, you are not the only one who forgets to answer them. As a matter of fact, most sales people are not very good at taking notes and most sales people are not very good at answering what they forgot to write down.

Wouldn't you like to be one of the few who do write the questions down and answer them promptly and properly? Just think for a moment how much credibility this would give you. If you complete this task properly all the time, you will win more sales and build better relationships than your competition.

Handling Messages

One more way to gain credibility through effective time management is to return your messages promptly. It doesn't matter if your customer left a message with your secretary or on a voice mail system or with a co-worker or any other means for that matter. Answer it quickly.

Why would your customer ever leave you a message if he knew you would not answer it? Think about this for a moment. How much credibility do you lose by not returning your phone messages in a timely manner? You lose credibility each and every time you ignore your customer.

Win Tip
Effective time management helps you focus.

We all know that your success depends largely on your credibility. There are many ways to gain or lose credibility with your customers. Effective time management helps you gain credibility and keep it. Organize yourself so you will enter their orders on time, address their questions and return their messages promptly and never be late for their meetings.

PLANNING

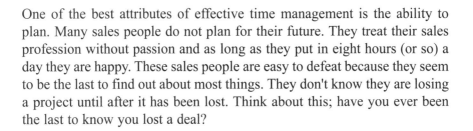

One of the best attributes of effective time management is the ability to plan. Many sales people do not plan for their future. They treat their sales profession without passion and as long as they put in eight hours (or so) a day they are happy. These sales people are easy to defeat because they seem to be the last to find out about most things. They don't know they are losing a project until after it has been lost. Think about this; have you ever been the last to know you lost a deal?

All through this book you will read about how important it is to set goals. Effective time management helps us set optimistic goals with proper time frames. It's hard to be successful in this profession if you don't have goals. Without goals and a process to achieve them, your competition will put you out of business in a hurry.

Setting Goals

There is an effective way to set goals. First, identify what you want to accomplish in the next week, month or year. Write these goals down and rank them in order of importance. Some of these goals might be volume increases over last year, or number of new customers in the next month, or to finish sales reports on time, and so on. You must decide what your goals will be. If you don't set any goals you will lose a lot of your effectiveness in sales campaigns.

Win Tip

What are you going to do next?

Sales Leaders set and achieve their goals. That's why they are the best. They do not settle for average performance from themselves. Now that you have decided you want to be a Sales Leader you must follow their direction.

A few years ago I was part of a large sales team in the insurance industry. You could ask any of the top sales people where their next five sales were going to come from and they almost always had an answer for you because through good time management they were able to gain control of their sales destinies.

When you asked the same question to the average sales people on the team they usually did not have an answer, however, they were quick to tell you they were busy dealing with stuff and working on things. It always seemed they never quite knew what stuff or things that they were working on but they had lots of it to do.

PERFORMANCE

Effective time management is much more than setting appointments and trying not to be late for them. Effective time management is commitment, promises, goal setting, priorities, strategies, promptness, effective note taking and being organized.

I have watched sales people do everything right except when they came to time management. I then watched all their efforts go down the drain.

Sales Leaders can sell any product or service in any industry. Most customers don't buy product or low price. They buy you and your solutions. Don't just do some things right, do them all right.

Win Tip
Dedicated time management is a prerequisite for optimum performance.

I learned a long time ago that if my customers don't like me then I would fail in the sales arena. If I fail at time management then I fail at sales in general. Take the time to learn how to be effective in time management. When you use time management effectively you become more focused. The more focused you become the more sales victories you will enjoy.

You must know if you are creating business for your company or if you are just creating work. You must know if your sales make a profit or not. Can your management rely on you to bring in sales without the headaches? Are all your customers happy or are they upset because of broken promises or lack of commitment? Do your customers ever complain because your company can't execute on time? Is your company at fault for these things or is it the result of your lack of time management skills?

Summary

Effective time management enables you to be organized so you can complete all the important tasks first. It helps you gain credibility with your customers – and that is vital. It allows you to plan properly and set goals. Most importantly, it helps you perform to the best of your ability. In the sales industry there is a direct relationship between effective time management and performance. Effective time management is a tool you need to know and understand and use every day. Take the time to learn it and use it. Your sales career depends upon it.

Effective Time Management will help you gain prosperous relationships with your customers. You will build credibility and trust by being organized. Effective time management allows you to plan all your moves. It also allows you to organize and rank your tasks.

Win Process:
Effective Time Management

☑ Organized   When you are in control

☑ Planning   Setting priorities

☑ Performance   Level of acceptance

☑ Paperwork   File it away

☑ Scheduling Calendar A tool for planning

☑ Commitment   A promise to your customer

☑ Priority   Rank in order of importance

☑ Workspace   Home away from home

Win Notes: My Time

Use this page to assess how you manage your time. What are your strengths? Where do you need to improve?

5

Training

Training

5

Before we get into the different types of courses and the reasons for taking them, let me tell you something I am a strong believer in – what got me to where I am today is no longer good enough to get me where I need to be tomorrow.

It's true. The world and everything in it is changing faster than ever before. If you don't continually update your skills, you will be quickly passed by those who do.

I have watched many sales people attend numerous courses in their first few years in the profession. Through these courses they became better sales people and put more victories in the win column. But then something happened. For whatever reason, they thought they didn't need any more training. I guess they decided that after a few successes they knew everything. That was when these sales people and many more like them made the biggest mistake of their careers. It didn't take too long for them to get left behind.

Win Tip

Continuous training is a key factor of success.

I know two seasoned veterans who were successful through most of their early years in sales. One of them continued to take some type of training course every month or two. The other gentleman hadn't been on a training program for many years. Their sales campaigns were as different as night and day. It was quite obvious the second gentleman hadn't developed his selling skills. He would fight hard, but failing to advance his skill level over the years had cost him dearly.

My advice to all is this: If you are a rookie in this profession then one of your top priorities should be to attend as many sales training courses as possible. Don't ever stop learning because no matter how good you are, the day you stop learning is the day your competition starts catching up. If you are a seasoned veteran, my advice is don't ever think you know it all. You need to bear down and gain as much knowledge as you can in order to stay ahead.

ELRUDE

Elrude 5-1

Several years ago, when he first became a sales person, Elrude attended a sales training program. He has not been involved in any type of sales training since. His results quite obviously tell the truth. Elrude is not a very good sales person because he has not developed his skills. He has learned some bad habits that continually undermine his success.

Jack, on the other hand, has regularly attended personal development courses during his career. His results tell a story as well.

There are three areas of training that you should constantly be focusing on: Personality, Product and Sales. After twenty-five years of successful selling, I still regularly attend courses and, most importantly, I still learn new ideas that help me win more often.

PERSONALITY TRAINING

Customers prefer to buy from people they like. Not a big surprise, right? It may seem incredibly obvious, but there it is. What is a big surprise though is how many sales people repeatedly ignore this fact during their sales campaigns. The people customers like the most are the people they get along with the best. And the people they get along with best are the people they relate to the easiest. And the people they relate to the easiest are the people who treat them with respect. And the sales people who treat customers with respect know how each customer wants to be treated, and act accordingly.

If you don't know how to adjust your personality to deal with all your different customers then you are digging a deep hole for yourself. A hole you may never climb out of.

Win Tip
Pride yourself on your personality.

The first step in adjusting your personality is – taking off your shoes. Go ahead and do that now. Don't be scared because you will be taking your shoes off every day of your selling career, sometimes more than once in the same day. Maybe this sounds ridiculous to you. I am telling you now that if you don't take your shoes off regularly, you will not be successful in sales. OK, now you may ask why.

If you don't take your shoes off, how are you going to put on your customers' shoes? I'm sure you have heard the saying about putting yourself in someone else's shoes. You are a sales person and your job is to sell your products or services. It doesn't matter what we call ourselves – consultants, technical sales reps, account managers, advisors or any other name you want to dream up, but let's be real. We are sales people. Our job is to sell.

Our customer, on the other hand, is a person trying to buy something that will fill his or her need. They must be convinced your product is the best fit for their need. You may think your product is the best for your customer. However, they are comparing your product with your competitors' and there could be large differences. If you don't put yourself in your customer's shoes, you will never understand their view.

Win Tip
If you don´t take your shoes off, how are you going to get your customer´s on?

When your customer buys a product from your competition you may think it was a bad decision. Do you really think customers make bad decisions? No, they buy products or services from the sales person they like. And customers like sales people who take the time to understand them and their needs. The first step in gaining this type of relationship is to be able to wear your customer's shoes. What I am saying here is that you need to have a full understanding of your customer's views and why they make the decisions they do. You must understand their decision making process.

I know that you have more than one customer and I also know all these customers can't possibly have the same personality. Therefore, it is up to you to adjust and change your personality to best fit with each and every customer. I'm not telling you to be someone different. What I am saying is you have to be flexible when it comes to dealing with all your customers as individuals.

Win Tip
Don´t get left behind, keep up with your training.

There are many different types of training programs available that will teach you how easy it is to sell effectively to all your customers no matter how different they may be. Register yourself into one of these programs and learn how your customers make their decisions. Once you understand your customer, it's much easier to sell to them.

I once knew a salesperson a few years ago and I couldn't believe how he managed to stay in the sales profession as long as he did. Everything was his way or no way. When a customer didn't share the same views as him, he would argue to the point where sometimes the customer would ask him to leave. Then he would complain and say his customer was stupid for not buying from him. Later he would go out of his way trying to prove his customers' decision was wrong.

Your job as a sales person is quite simple – understand what the customer wants to buy and provide the solution. If you're following the right process, there are not many ways to screw things up. It amazes me how many sales people go out of their way to invent ways to screw up a sale. Why argue with a customer? How is that ever going to help you win a sale?

Have you ever gone on a sales call and when the meeting was completed you thought it was very positive for you? Do you ever wonder what the customers' perception of that meeting was? Have you ever asked your customer what they thought, after the meeting was completed? At the end of your next sales meeting, ask your customer to level with you and tell you exactly how they think the meeting went. Ask them what they liked about the meeting and ask them what they didn't like about it. When they tell you what they didn't like about the meeting, ask them why. This will be a humbling experience for you but constructive feedback never hurt anyone and it shouldn't hurt you either.

Win Tip

Don't invent new ways to screw up a sale. They will happen naturally.

You will be amazed at what you will find out about yourself when you do this. I pride myself on my personality. As a matter of fact I think my personality is my strongest selling feature. I constantly look for feedback on my personality by asking my customers how I handle myself while I am with them. I do the same with my co-workers. I love their responses. Good constructive feedback is healthy for the soul. Let me caution you though, you may not like some things you hear.

Don't ever ask your customer what they thought and than jump all over them because they didn't give you the answer you wanted to hear. If you do, I guarantee it will be the last time you will ever deal with that customer.

The importance here is that you need to be flexible when it comes to your personality. The more you can be like your customer, the more customers you will have and the more these customers will like you. When a customer likes you, more business will most assuredly come your way.

Your personality is one of your strongest tools. There are reasons why some sales people are Sales Leaders while others struggle. Whether you do everything else right or wrong, not being able to bring a personality that is flexible and non-aggressive to the table will keep you from the success you deserve.

I know you want to be better than you are today. You probably would not have bought this book if you felt otherwise. As you read this book you will find many ways how you can improve your sales efforts but none are more important than working on your personality. Your customers will read your personality within minutes of meeting you for the first time. This is when they make a decision whether they will ever buy from you.

To attain the personality that will make you successful you must practice different methods of expression. Talk to your family, friends and co-workers and ask them how you come across during conversations with them. Ask them if you are opinionated, or aggressive. These are the two types of people that usually have problems in the sales profession. Customers don't really care about your opinion, you're not buying – they are. They also don't like ideas being rammed down their throats.

There is one secret to always remember when dealing with people: be nice. If you can just be nice, everything else will fall into place. When you are nice, your customers like you more and will trust you more because you are too nice to lie to them and too nice to lead them in a direction they shouldn't venture. When you gain your customers' trust, you are on the road to great success. Be nice and have a nice personality. When you can show your customers that everything you do comes from your heart, they will be your customers forever.

PRODUCT TRAINING

Contrary to some sales people's beliefs, you do need to know something about what you are selling. On the other hand, knowing too much can be dangerous.

There are basically three types of sales people. There are sales people who know nothing about their product or service but are good at building relationships. They tend to be somewhat successful. There are sales people who know most things about their product or service, everything about their company's products that is not available anymore and most things about their competitor's products. These sales people are so busy focusing on products, they have no time left in their day to work on anything else. Their relationship building is virtually non-existent. The success rate of this type of sales person is usually low. The third group is made up of sales people who know a few things about their products and are quite good at relationship building. You will find most of the Sales Leaders in this group.

Win Tip

Be prepared to change jobs internally or externally to advance your career.

Some sales people have the ability to build relationships with anyone. Customers can be convinced to actually buy from these sales people. The difficulty that arises with sales people like this is they are usually successful until a problem or issue arises. When this happens, these types of sales people often have trouble solving the problem. They do not know enough about the product or service they are selling to understand the issue from the customer's perspective. Their relationship abilities are overshadowed by their lack of knowledge about the very product or service they are selling.

The most dangerous sales person is the one who knows too much about the inner workings of their product. The reason why they are dangerous is because all they want to do is to show the customer these inner workings. The most important thing to them is to make sure their customer understands as much about the product as they do. They talk so much that many times they talk themselves out of the sale.

Let's look at an example of the product-focused sales person. You set out to buy a new car and you have given yourself a couple of model choices. You visit several dealerships and get a rundown on the models you are looking at and you even go for a test drive or two. At one dealership a sales person relentlessly follows you. Once he gets your attention, you become his student. As you plan your escape route, you learn everything from tire sizes to fan belts, from the origin of steel to a geography lesson about which country produces the best engine oil.

As time passes, you finally break free and run out the front door, hoping you didn't forget anything while you were there. It's too bad, you think to yourself, because that was a nice car. You will just have to find another one like it at a different dealership.

This happens in almost every industry and it happens more than it should. This type of sales person agitates customers. They don't use common sense, they don't know how to build relationships and they don't know how to communicate properly. All they do is talk about their product. I'm not saying that too much product training can make you a product-focused sales person. What I am saying is there is a limit to how much product knowledge you should have.

The most successful sales person is the one who knows their product or service from a technical point of view and are good at building relationships. When any issue arises, these sales people are able to quickly repair the issue in a win-win scenario for both the customer and their own company. Their strong relationship abilities coupled with their technical knowledge ensures a quick resolution that keeps their customer happy.

Through good product training courses you should be in a position where you can confidently demonstrate and operate the product well enough to cover all the features and benefits your customers are interested in. You should know this for all your major products. You should also have an understanding of all the other products your company sells.

Another important area of product training comes from knowing what your competition is selling. You must have a good understanding of all your competitors' offerings. This can be difficult but if you are creative you can find many ways to obtain information about your competitors' products. I can think of three ways to obtain this information: ask your customers, ask your competition, or download the information from your competition's website.

Product information is important for your customer. Without knowing what your product can do, it will be tough for anyone to decide whether or not to buy it. What is important for you is to know how to get this information to your customer. There are always people within your company who know your product feature-for-feature. You build the relationships and bring these

people in to explain the inner workings of your product. I think you will find this to be a successful campaign.

SALES TRAINING

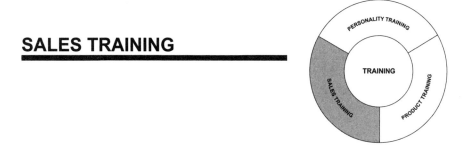

There is an old saying about sales people not being taught or trained; they are, in fact, born as sales people. Well, that statement doesn't have much truth to it. That's why there are just as many (or possibly more) sales courses available then there are product courses.

Many years ago people thought good sales people were born with the gift of the gab, which simply means they knew how to talk. Only recently we have come to realize the best sales people don't talk a lot. So, why are things different today compared to a decade or two ago? Maybe things haven't changed. Maybe we just thought good sales people talked a lot when in fact the listeners were winning the big sales.

However, there is more to selling than just talking or listening. We must accept the fact that in the twenty first century the best sales people will be the best trained sales people. The old gift of the gab just won't cut it anymore.

There are basically two different types of sales courses. The first type I call the honest and ethical course. This type of training teaches you to win by using your own intelligence, strategies and tactics. When you are successful at achieving victory in a sales campaign it is even more rewarding to know you won fair and square and your entire campaign was based on honesty.

The second type of sales course I call how to set up my customer to buy from me. Stay away from this type of course. It can ruin your career. Basically, this type of course teaches you how to set up your customer by asking loaded questions. You end up pinning your customer in a corner and selling something he or she doesn't want or need. Once you have attended a few of these courses, you will walk around with a pocket full of the wrong closes and you will see many doors close in your face.

How can you tell a good course from a bad one? First, you have to look at who is offering the course. If they are not recognized or well known, then you should look deeper. Secondly, watch out for the price. When you are in desperate need of sales training you probably don't have much spare cash sitting around to enroll in a course. Usually good courses cost more, but when that is all you can afford, a poor/cheap course is better than nothing right? Wrong. Dead wrong.

You are better off buying a good book on selling and spending time reading the material rather than enrolling in a course that will potentially make you worse off then you are today. These bargain-priced courses may sound great at first but don't get caught in their scheme. These people are not in business to make you better, they are in business to make money for themselves and that's all.

What you learn becomes what you use every day thereafter on your sales campaigns so make sure you learn the right material. There are many great trainers who will teach you what you need to know to be a Sales Leader. You must find these people and learn from them.

Win Tip
Re-read, Re-Listen and Re-attend.

Read their books, listen to their tapes and attend their seminars. I mentioned earlier that I have been in the sales profession for twenty-five years and I still read their books, listen to their tapes and attend their seminars. Each time I re-read, re-listen or re-attend, I learn something new. My strongest competitors do this as well. I can tell by their strategies when I compete against them. Sales training is extremely important so make sure you get involved and learn as much as you can. Your future success depends on it.

ELRUDE

Jack Coleman has been working hard for the last few months trying to close a large project for his company. It has become quite a complex selling process involving many people and a large number of meetings.

Jack is up for the challenge of course and has made all the right steps to gain the control he needs to be successful. While Jack is meeting with his customer and building his strategy, he has also booked himself into a one-day training seminar, right in the middle of his selling campaign. Jack has thought about not attending.

Finally, at the last minute, Jack decides to attend this seminar entitled 'Knowing your Competition.' He feels that even though the timing doesn't fit his schedule perfectly, he should still be there.

Jack attends and is amazed at what happens. First, he notices several of his competitors at the same seminar. Also, on this project he is chasing he knows he has four competitors, and two of them are at this seminar! He now understands who will be his strongest competition. Jack knows if he gets something out of this seminar that his competitors don't, he could gain an advantage.

Jack continually keeps an eye on his two competitors while trying to absorb as much new content as possible. He notices one competitor keeps dozing off, only to wake with a snap of his head every few minutes. Obviously, he wasn't learning very much.

As the day progresses Jack is attentive and listens for anything he can use to gain an advantage. Shortly after lunch it happens. Something the instructor is talking about triggers Jack to think about his customer. Jack quickly forms a question around this thought and believes the answer will put him in a better position for the victory. He watches his competitors, who are now both nodding off into dreamland.

When the seminar concludes, Jack quickly rushes out and calls his customer, asking the question he had formed earlier in the day. When he receives his answer he is now confident the lowest price is not going to win. As a matter of fact, he now knows the lowest price submitted will automatically be discarded. This customer has a policy to discard the lowest and the highest bids.

Across town, Elrude Noclue was chasing the same project. He met with his customer a few times but usually over-stayed his welcome, which only lasted about 10 minutes each visit. Elrude did not attend the sales seminar that Jack Coleman had because he felt the fee was too high. Besides, Elrude had a plan. This time he was going to be the lowest price and he would be victorious for sure.

Elrude 5-2

Elrude did not involve anyone else in the selling process for this particular project. When his boss asked him details about the project Elrude deflected the questions and provided vague answers. His boss knew Elrude really doesn't have a clue about his position on this project but he told himself he would give Elrude a year no matter what happened. There are only a couple of months left before the decision will be executed. Elrude is fortunate to have a boss that is comfortable giving him this much time. Usually sales managers cannot afford to be so lenient.

Elrude hasn't taken a sales course since his first year in the profession and feels what he learns on the street will benefit him more than what he could possibly learn in a classroom. His boss tried to explain the difference to Elrude about two people, one who goes to school and one who doesn't.

The project was awarded a few days later and both Elrude Noclue and Jack Coleman waited patiently for the decision. Jack was in complete control and was not surprised in the least when he was told he had won. Elrude was totally shocked when he discovered he had lost. He even got into a heated dispute with the customer because he did have the lowest price but was thrown out early. There was no thought put in that decision Elrude complained, thinking this customer shafted him.

Jack Coleman's customer shook his head in disbelief at the response he received from Elrude. He wondered if Elrude had ever won a project.

Summary

There are many types of training programs that can help you become a Sales Leader. These include product training, personality training, effective communication training and general sales training. There are courses on speaking, presenting, prospecting and competitive product knowledge. There are expensive courses and cheap courses, long-term courses and short-term courses as well as in-house courses and external courses. Commit to personal improvement by taking advantage of these offerings.

The forgotten art of **Training** takes its toll on many great sales people. You must continue to fill your training needs throughout your entire career. Good training will keep your knowledge level current and it can even offer you a strong advantage in some of your sales campaigns.

Win Process: Training

☑ Advantage   Something training gives you

☑ Customers' shoes   Put them on

☑ Personality   You must have a positive one

☑ Courses   Attend the good ones

☑ Selling   What this is all about

☑ Product   Something you are selling

☑ Service   Something else you are selling

☑ Personal Development   Your own growth plan

Win Notes: My Training

Use this page to assess your skill and knowledge levels. What are your strengths? Where do you need to improve?

6   Excitement

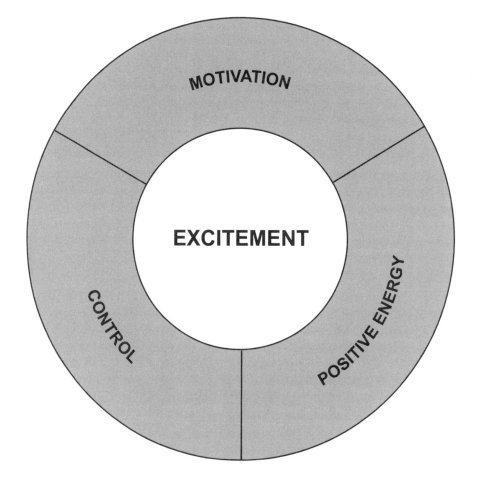

Excitement

6

Successful sales people are exciting. But are they exciting because they are successful or are they successful because they are exciting? Becoming a Sales Leader requires you to complete many small tasks well, all of the time. Adding excitement to your day is one of those tasks.

Excitement works in conjunction with common sense, relationship building and product knowledge. You must understand how to communicate this excitement in order to be effective.

Excitement is the ice cream on top of the pie. It is the sizzle of the steak. It is the benefit, not the feature. Excitement increases your chances of winning any sale as long as you cover the other bases as well. I must warn you though; excitement alone will not win a sale. As a matter of fact, excitement alone might create problems for you. When you are excited, you sometimes talk more. We discussed the downfalls of talking too much earlier in this book.

There are three main categories related to excitement: motivation, positive energy and control.

MOTIVATION

Learn to smile. Learn to say hello, goodbye and thank-you. Learn to ask basic questions like, how are you today? Learn to be happy. When you are happy and smiling it motivates your customer to smile back at you. Making your customers smile opens another door for you as well. People enjoy smiling and they quite often remember what or who made them smile.

Win Tip
Successful people are exciting.

Remember that your customer must know and like you before he or she will buy from you. Customers will buy the product anyway. The only remaining decision is from which company and which sales person. If you are motivated enough, you could be that successful sales person.

There are a number of ways to become, and just as importantly, stay motivated. It's tough to be motivated when you are not happy. When you enjoy your work you tend to be motivated. When you are motivated in your sales career, you become more successful, which could result in promotions, which usually mean more income, which makes you happier and in turn drives you to be more motivated. This circle continues throughout your entire career.

Now, let's say that you have become happy in your profession and you are internally motivated to strive to the next level of your career. This motivation drives your daily habits. Instead of just talking about your product to customers, you present it to your customers. Your personality changes to be more open, flexible and exciting.

Win Tip
Nice guys finish first.

Your customers will like dealing with you, and as we've said before, customers buy from people they like. When they find your are easy to do business with, because you are more open and flexible, they will become excited to do business with you. Now you have reached a stage where your motivation for selling is influencing your customer to be motivated to buy from you. This is the position we should always be working toward.

There are two steps to motivation. The first is learning to become motivated and the second is learning to stay motivated. There is one very easy way to become motivated but unfortunately many sales people bypass this method. Keep your tasks simple and go where the rewards are. Let's face it, the more successful you become, the more reason you have to be motivated. The more motivated you are, the more successful you can become.

The first step toward successful motivation is making sure you complete only those tasks related directly to your success. Don't clutter your day with tasks that are not taking you directly to your next sale. When you add extra tasks to your busy day, you are in fact adding more activities that could have less than a positive impact on your sales results and your motivation. The end goal is to sell more and create more victories for you and your company.

Win Tip

Winning sales is your only function.

How long do you think you would stay motivated if you never closed any sales? Your job as a sales person is to get those victories. For the most part your supervisor doesn't really care how. As long as you are ethical, he or she will just care how many.

Take a few moments to re-evaluate your efforts. Stop doing tasks that are not taking you closer to getting that order. You can become motivated only if you are working directly toward your next victory. You are a sales person and winning sales is your only function. Sales Leaders don't complicate their days with non-productive tasks. They focus only on those tasks that contribute to their sales success. That is their driving force.

POSITIVE ENERGY

When you are positive, you have the power of success at your fingertips. When you are negative, you are well on you way to having nearly nothing. Sales Leaders are some of the most positive people you will ever meet.

Being positive is a state of mind. The first rule you should make for yourself is to think only positive thoughts. When you continually think positive thoughts and ideas, an amazing new world will open in front of your eyes. You will walk with purpose, not resignation. You will speak with conviction, not apprehension. You will think like a winner, not act like a victim. You will challenge yourself to always do better.

In most cases, when a customer tells you no, what it really means is that he or she isn't sure. When you continually think positive you will recognize that your customer is not really saying no, but in fact is asking you to help him better understand your offer. People who are not positive simply walk away from the sale the first time the customer says no. Remain positive when your customer first uses that two-letter word. It can have a big impact on your career and your life.

Winning is in the way you present it. You can be positive and successful or negative and fail. Make a commitment to yourself right now to be positive in all that you do, and see how it changes everything.

CONTROL

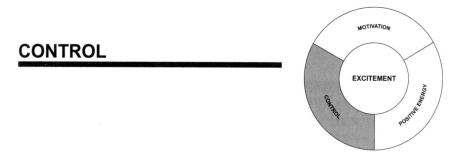

You always need to be in control of your sales campaign. Whenever there is a sale in progress someone is in control. Usually, that someone, is victorious in the end. Shouldn't that be you? Of course it should and that is why we need control. Let's look at a simple example that happens in everyday life.

You and your companion decide on the weekend that you will go out for dinner and a movie. Your companion offers to make all the arrangements. When the weekend arrives you go out and feast on a great meal but in your eyes, the movie was not very good. You wished you had seen a different one playing at the same cinema. Your companion also thought the dinner was delicious and enjoyed the movie as well.

Now, the result was you and your companion spent a pleasant evening together. However, you did not organize the events of the evening;

therefore, you had no control in picking the movie. This put you in a position of not watching the movie you really wanted to see. You had no control in setting up the event.

When you have no control, you lack the power to affect the end decision. In the sales profession you need to have this power. If you don't have control over the direction of the decision then you could be in big trouble. I must add there are instances where an individual might not be in a position of control but they are in a position of influence with the person in control. This can sometimes be leveraged as well.

ELRUDE

Because of his excitable personality, Elrude Noclue tends to stand out from the crowd and people notice whatever he does and says. The product Elrude is selling is now more expensive than the product his competition is offering. Elrude's company

Elrude 6-1

has just increased the price of the product twice in the last three months. It's also a better product. He starts his sales call by telling his customer his product is now more expensive than whatever his competition is offering. Elrude explains he has been telling his manager this since the day the first price increase came about, but no discounting has been allowed. Elrude goes on to say even he wouldn't buy his product at this price.

> Elrude continues by telling his customer that his company can't seem to sell any at this price and may need to downsize because of it. Elrude's customer stops him and makes a statement that he thought Elrude's product was the best on the market. Elrude replies yes but reverts back to his price now being too high.

Now, let's talk about how you get this control. It comes from being focused. It also comes from being motivated as well. When you start a sales campaign you must be loyal to your tasks. If you miss a step along the way, you could lose some of your control in the campaign. We know there are many different tasks in a given sales campaign and it is your responsibility to include all of them. I have been involved in sales campaigns where there are as little as two or three tasks and I have also been involved in a sales campaign where there were 316 tasks over a ten month period.

Win Tip

If you are not in control of your sales campaign – who is?

Through your motivation for victory and your dedication for completing all your tasks you can maintain the control you need. Stay on top of the campaign. Apply yourself and focus on getting that victory. Don't start into a sales campaign unless you plan on winning.

Summary

The message I want to leave you with is this – be as successful as you can. If you enjoy your work you will be more successful than those who don't. When you enjoy your work you become more excited. So when you get up in the morning and prepare yourself for your day, be positive, be motivated, be in control, be focused and show all your customers how excitement will guarantee you catch their sale.

Excitement alone will not win for you, but without it, you could lose. Excitement is a derivative of motivation. Excitement and finely tuned sales skills can place you at the top of the Sales Leader board quickly. Excitement allows you to pursue the challenges that lie ahead, and plan for the forthcoming victories.

Win Process: Excitement

☑ Motivation	Your inner driving force
☑ Control	Yours to lose, so don't
☑ Positive Energy	Power of success
☑ Happy	When you smile
☑ Thank You	Never said enough
☑ Sizzle	An exciting benefit
☑ First	Where you should be
☑ Winning	Your only function

Win Notes: My Excitement

Use this page to assess your level of excitement and how you project this to your customers. What are your strengths? Where do you need to improve?

Section 1: Learning the Game

Summary

Learning to be a sales person is a prerequisite to being hired as a sales person.

Imagine for a moment you are a manager. Would you hire a welder who could not weld? Would you hire a truck driver who could not drive? Would you hire a cook who could not cook? What about a sales person who doesn't know how to sell? Would you ever hire one of those people? Of course you wouldn't.

In order to become a Sales Leader you need to work on a solid foundation.

Create an image that is both professional and personable. Develop a positive attitude and bring an element of common sense to the playing field. Learn to communicate effectively through listening and understanding. Be organized and develop your time management skills. Adopt the attitude that continuous training is important. Finally, pump yourself up for an exciting career.

Sales Leaders learn the game before they practice it.

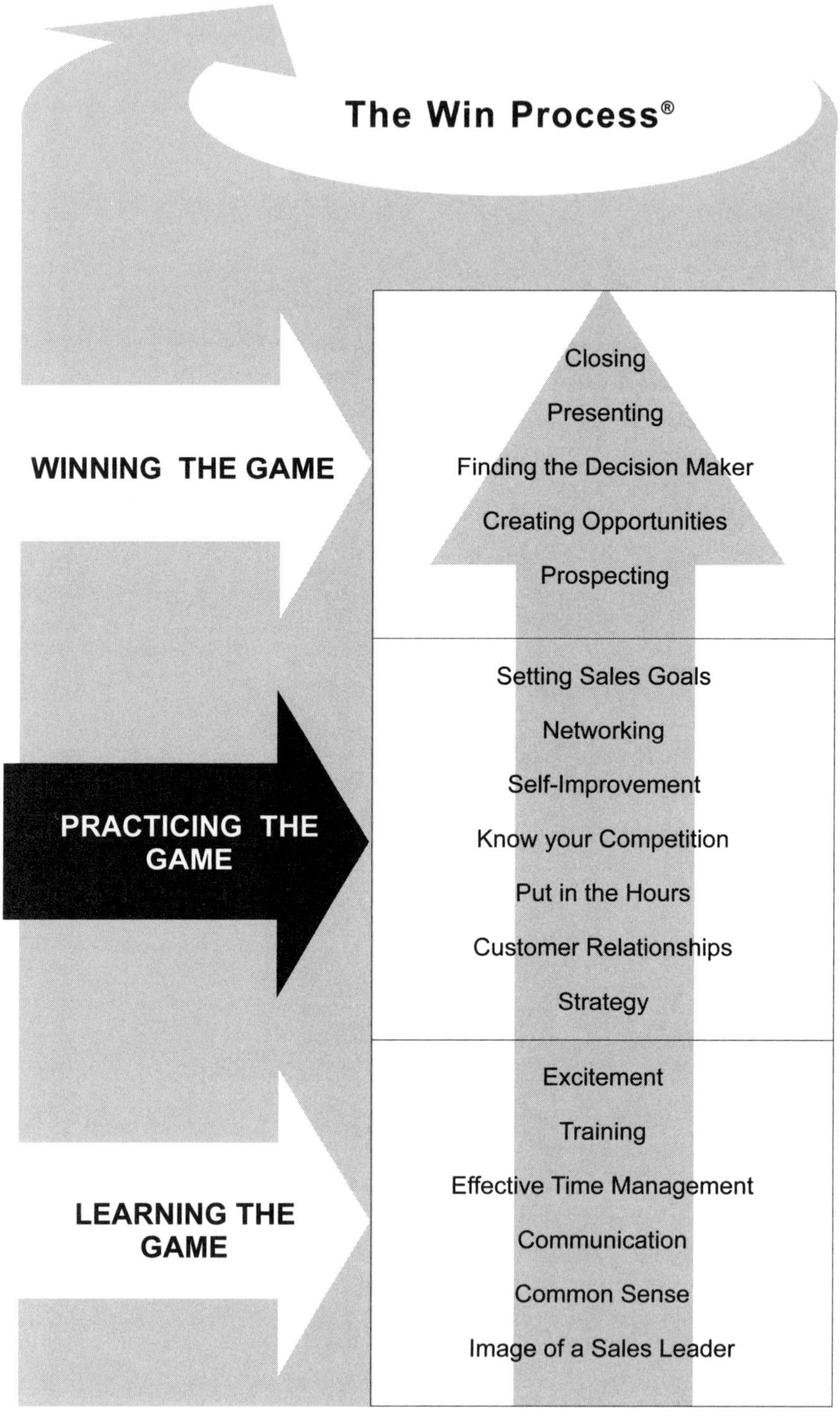

The Win Process®

WINNING THE GAME

Closing

Presenting

Finding the Decision Maker

Creating Opportunities

Prospecting

PRACTICING THE GAME

Setting Sales Goals

Networking

Self-Improvement

Know your Competition

Put in the Hours

Customer Relationships

Strategy

LEARNING THE GAME

Excitement

Training

Effective Time Management

Communication

Common Sense

Image of a Sales Leader

Section 2: Practicing the Game

Introduction

Now that you have adopted the behaviors of a Sales Leader, you must to practice and develop these actions. Section 2 deals with applying your new skills in your day-to-day activities.

Mastering this section will be demonstrated by your ability to:

- Build a **Strategy** for controlling your activities
- Leverage **Customer Relationships** to assist your sales efforts
- **Put in the Hours** necessary to do what needs to be done
- **Know Your Competition** and take them by surprise
- Commit to personal and professional **Self-Improvement**
- Utilize **Networking** for personal and business development
- Move your personal and business yardsticks by **Setting Sales Goals**

7   Strategy

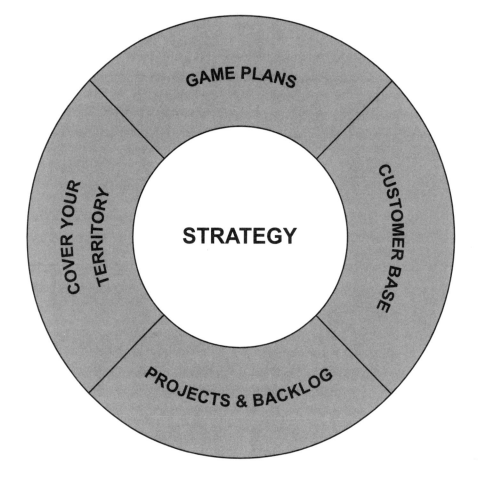

Strategy

7

Now it is time to move on and start practicing because it won't be long before you are generating sale after sale. Let's start by building a strategy. First though, we need to understand what a strategy is and why we would use one.

A strategy is a plan. No matter what task you take on in life, you need a plan. Some plans are simple and consist of only one step. These are easy to implement because you know the plan thoroughly in your head. An example would be taking the garbage to the curb. You grab the bag of garbage, open the door and walk to the curb dropping the bag as you turn back to the house. Most people would take on this task anytime because it is a simple one with minimal planning.

Win Tip

Winging it is your quickest ticket out of the selling profession.

What if your next task was to build a bookshelf? This task is more complex and requires more thought and preparation. In either the case, you are planning.

Some sales people assume they don't need to build a strategy. They feel it is a waste of time. They feel they can just go out there and sell. Interestingly enough though, many of these sales people discover they can't seem to win anything. That process is called winging it, and sales people who sell this way are usually looking for work in another industry after a short stint in the sales profession.

There are other parts to strategy than just planning. In this chapter we will look at all aspects of strategy so you will know what to practice and why. First we will talk about building game plans and setting goals. We will discuss your customer base, or your potential customer base if you are just starting. Also, we will discuss projects and get a clear understanding of what a backlog is and why it is important to have a big one. Finally, we will talk about how to cover your territory and see all your customers. We have lots to cover so let's get started.

GAME PLANS

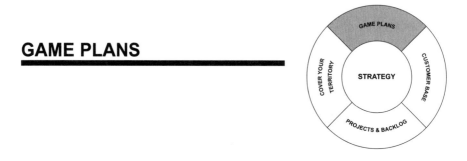

You've read the first section of this book, Learning The Game, and are ready to begin or transform your sales career. So what are you going to do now? When you walk into your office tomorrow morning, do you know right now what will be your first task? I bet you don't.

This is the root of the problem and if you can't answer the questions above, then it is time for a change in your planning approach. Sales people who do not plan usually let their work control them instead of the other way around. Quick review from the previous chapter: Who needs to have control? You do and when you do, you will win more times.

You must be in control of what you do each day. This includes what tasks should be completed, what meetings need to be attended, what paperwork needs to be finished, what phone calls need to be made and what e-mails need to be read and actioned.

If you were to take your own poll and ask several sales people what they do from the minute they get out of bed on a workday until they arrive back home for supper, you will be amazed at what you learn. Tell them you want the full truth about each time they took a break or worked on something that was not taking them closer to a sales victory. Once you have completed this poll and have examined the data, you decide if they are in control of their activities or if their work is controlling them.

One simple way to tell if you are in control is this – if the first thing you do every morning you arrive at the office is turn on your computer and read all your new e-mails, (jokes included), you are probably letting your work control you.

ELRUDE

Elrude Noclue was not a planner. When he walked into his office each morning he never knew what he would be doing. He spent his entire day in a reactive mode letting his work dictate his time. Elrude never made a telephone cold call in his life and his results proved it. Whenever his co-workers asked what he was working on, Elrude always responded he

Aaaahhh! This is the third time today!

Elrude 7-1

was working on a lot of stuff and things. He was constantly busy, he thought.

Some Saturdays Elrude would make three or four trips to the grocery store. He would never write a list and plan for just one trip. He thought planning took too long. He felt he could be to the store and back before other people finished their planning. Elrude never considered how much time the other trips would take him, yet he felt he never had enough time on the weekend to get the things done that he needed.

Elrude approached his workdays in the same fashion. He could never figure out where all the time went. While he was up to his eyeballs in stuff and things, his competition kept on winning.

Once when I was evaluating why my closing rate was higher than other people I was working with, I uncovered an amazing result. It made me investigate other sales people outside my company and again to my amazement the same results occurred. Many sales people don't plan. I couldn't believe it. This investigation gave me the best ammunition I could ever ask for. All I had to do from that day on when building my plan was to allow for my competition to not build a plan. I thought selling was easy before, now I believe it is a piece of cake.

Let's now discuss how to build a game plan. Each one will be different and customized to whatever you are selling but there are a few basics that will make up the core of any game plan.

Take a blank sheet of paper and, on the left side of the page, randomly write down every task you feel needs to be completed in order for you to be successful in winning the next sale. It doesn't matter if the ideas are good or bad. All we want to do now is let your mind work at generating ideas.

Don't put them in order of when you feel they should be completed. We will do that later. All you have to do now is write down ideas that your mind generates. Make sure you write every idea down on paper, even the simple and easy ones. These are sometimes overlooked if not written down.

Win Tip

Do not complicate matters with extra steps.

You never know when you might generate an idea which, at the start, seemed crazy but the more you thought about it the more you liked it. This is called brainstorming. This is the reason why we write down the bad ideas as well as the good ones. Some bad ideas turn out to be real winners because in writing those down we had time to think about them a bit more. Our creative minds work harder to fine-tune these ideas until one day we tweak and twist the bad idea enough that it becomes a great idea and actually helps us win a sale we are chasing.

For those of you who are familiar with planning, you will probably have little problem writing down ten or fifteen different tasks that need to become part of your selling strategy. For those of you who are not, this may be a difficult exercise. Once you start planning and continue to plan every day, this exercise becomes easier and will result in more sales for you. Let's look at a few generic examples:

TASK LIST

■ Set up meetings to ensure you know exactly who your customer is.

■ Ask your customer questions to gain an understanding on what they want to buy.

■ Ask your customer when they plan to make their purchase.

■ Ask your customer how much they want to spend or what their budget is for this purchase.

■ Ask your customer who you are competing with.

■ Ask around your own company to see if anyone is available to help you on this sales campaign.

■ Ask any outside acquaintances if they would be willing to help you if you need them.

■ Talk with your manager to see if there is any strength within your company that may put you in a better position for victory (maybe this customer already purchased from your company in the past).

■ Talk with your manager to see if there is any weakness within your company that may hurt your chances for victory (maybe this customer had a bad experience with your company in the past).

■ Ask your customer how they will make their decision about what they plan to buy.

It is important not to restrict your mind when you are unleashing its power to generate ideas. That is why you should never ask yourself for good ideas only. Get all the ideas out and make sure you write them down. Many people tell me they have fantastic memories and they do not need to use pen and paper. These people are only kidding themselves because none of them have ever convinced me they can remember all the tasks that need to be completed.

Once you have completed writing down all your tasks, use the right side of the page to write down all the goals you can think of as well. There are many goals that need to be listed and if you don't write them down you will have trouble measuring the end result. How will you know if you succeeded or not? Your goals are just as important as your tasks. Some examples of goals in relation to the above examples of tasks are:

GOALS LIST

- Find out who your customer is. (Date to be completed)
- Find out what your customer wants to buy. (Date to be completed)
- Find out when your customer wants to buy. (Date to be completed)
- Find out how much your customer wants to pay for what they plan to buy. (Date to be completed)
- Find out who your competition is. (Date to be completed)
- Find out who in your company will help you. (Date to be completed)
- Find out who outside your company will help you. (Date to be completed)
- Find out your customer's decision making criteria (low price, most features, etc.) (Date to be completed)
- Find out your company's strengths that can help you win. (Date to be completed)
- Find out your company's weaknesses that could hurt your chances of winning. (Date to be completed)

Now, let's go back to your tasks and put them in order of when you think they should be completed. Don't put dates or times down yet. We only want to generate the order in which they need to be completed for now. Here's an example. Your task is to call the customer and ask him what date he plans to make his purchase. Your goal here is to find out from the customer when he will buy. When he gives you the answer of next Wednesday, you have attained that particular goal.

Now you can set up more tasks between today and next Wednesday so you can be in position to accept an order when he is ready to give it. When you complete a task and achieve the goal associated with it, you are now prepared to generate more tasks and goals and so on until you win the sale in the end.

What would happen if you did not write down your tasks and the thought of calling your customer to ask when he will buy did not occur to you until next Thursday? The answer is quite simple, actually. You would have lost the sale and the reason would be lack of planning. The sale would have already been awarded to someone else.

The final two steps of building a game plan are, first, to put dates to all the tasks now that you have them in the proper order and then execute these tasks. That in a nutshell is a game plan.

Reviewing the game plan, we start off by listing all the tasks that must be completed and attaching goals to each and every task. Then we put the tasks in order and apply dates to them. Then we execute, always keeping in mind to attain the goal that is associated with each task. Please remember to write all this information down on paper. Once you do this you are well on your way to a more successful career than if you didn't plan your strategy. Always know what you are going to do next. Walking into the office every morning with nothing planned does two things for you. It causes you grief and it causes you to be stressed. Stress is a catalyst for a stroke or a heart attack.

CUSTOMER BASE

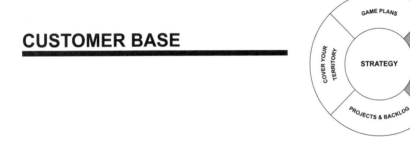

You must have a customer base in order to sell. Some of you will be lucky enough to work with companies that already have a base of customers. Others will need to start from scratch and build a customer base from the ground up. I have been in both situations more than once throughout my sales career and although having a customer base to work with is easier, sometimes it is better to start on the ground floor and make your own.

There are three important questions you need to answer and be able to continually answer when looking at your customer base. Who is your customer base? Where is your customer base? What is your customer base buying today?

Who is your customer?

First, let's look at your customer base – present and future. A customer is any person or company that buys, or may buy, a product or service from you or your competition. All the names that fall into this category will be your customer base. It is up to you to increase the amount of customers in your base as fast as you can. The more people or companies you add to your customer base will have an impact on your future sales volumes.

When a person or company buys from you and you execute everything right, they should always be your customer. There may be times where they don't buy much but there will also be times when they will buy a lot.

Win Tip

A good customer base is a strong foundation.

It is your job to increase your sales numbers regularly if you want to become a Sales Leader. One of the best ways to increase sales is to increase the amount of customers in your customer base. The other is to increase the amount of products/services your customers can buy from you.

Where is your customer base?

It can be anywhere. You should be creative enough to go out there and find it. The biggest mistake you could ever make is to sit back and wait for a potential customer to come looking for you – especially when your competition is out there actively calling on them. There is a customer base out there somewhere and many sales people from different companies are trying to obtain this base for themselves. It is up to you to get more than your share.

I said you should be creative to find a customer base but actually it goes further than that – you must be more creative than your competition.

There are many places to generate a customer base. Finding these places and building your own customer base requires a lot of work. You should operate just like a farmer when it comes time to plant crops. If they sow seeds sparingly they will have a small harvest later in the year. If they aggressively sow a large volume of seeds, they will reap large rewards by having a plentiful harvest.

There is an old saying – you get out of it what you put into it. If you don't build a solid customer base, chances are you will never become a Sales Leader. When you are building a house and you decide not to put much effort into the foundation, I wonder what could happen in a few years. You could wake up one morning and find yourself in the basement.

When looking for a customer base you must be open minded and willing to search anywhere. Depending on what industry you are selling in, you could use tools such as newspapers, radio, television, billboards, the Internet, the telephone, your company's existing files, referral services or marketing directories. Whatever the case, you must go get the customer base. Don't wait for it to come to you.

Win Tip

You will get out of it what you put into it.

Let me talk for a moment about one sales industry where there is a false feeling that a customer base will come to the sales person. This industry is automobile sales and I don't want to single them out but they represent a good example for what I need to explain.

I know many automotive sales people who spend the entire day waiting in their office for customers to walk in the door. Their sales results are average or below average. Compare this with the few sales people who actively go out looking for business.

Sure they still have to work their shift on the showroom floor but they don't spend all of that time waiting for people who may or may not come in. They already have appointments set up with people who are interested in buying from them. Their entire shift is full of meaningful sales activities, whereas the ones who wait for customers to walk in the door spend lots of time reading the newspaper and drinking coffee. Who do you think will make more sales and more money?

Let's look at the same situation in a different light. The dealership has just launched a new truck promotion, supported by newspaper advertising and radio commercials. The average sales person waits in his office all day long for customers to walk in but only a few people pass through the showroom. Of these, none were looking for a truck so it was like a regular business day in his mind. The Sales Leader decided he would be creative so he made copies of the newspaper ad, taped the radio commercials onto a blank cassette and signed out a new, fully loaded truck and drove out to the country. He went from farm to farm showing people the new truck on promotion this month.

While these potential buyers were looking at the truck, the cassette was playing the radio commercials. Before he left each farm he gave the farmer a copy of the newspaper ad with his business card stapled to it. As well, the sales person asked the farmer if he knew anyone in the area who was looking for a new truck.

How do you think each sales person did at the end of the day? The average sales person spent all his time in his office at the showroom. He read the entire newspaper and drank many cups of coffee. He saw twelve people that came through the showroom of which only two were serious shoppers. Of these two, one was price shopping on a subcompact car and the other was looking for full size car to compare to one he saw at another dealership. The average sales person made no sales, set up no appointments and received no commitments from any customer that they would be returning.

The Sales Leader spent all his time driving from farm to farm. He rarely had time to drink coffee and he had no time to read the paper. He was out in the fresh air all day and had lots of fun. He visited twelve farms and generated interest on six of his visits. Every farm he visited already owned trucks ranging from almost new to over ten years old. He made no sales but he set up four appointments and two of these potential customers were quite interested in doing business with him because he showed interest in having them as a customer.

This activity was repeated each day of the truck promotion. At the end of the month the average sales person had two sales and not much money because he gave away most of the profit to get those sales. He has no leads for next month so his excitement level is low. He is unmotivated and complains about his job. Eventually he will move on where he will do the same at another dealership.

The Sales Leader sold ten new trucks, each at a reasonable profit. He is excited about his job and can't wait for next month because he already has seven appointments set up from all his excursions outside the showroom.

An interesting point to make is these two sales people started off at exactly the same point on the first day of the month. One sowed seeds sparingly while the other was aggressively sowing volume. The results were dramatically different. Now take a moment to think how this applies in your industry.

What is your customer buying?

Find out what your customers need and provide it for them. Make it as easy as you can for them to buy and they will become your customer.

Customers buy for a variety of reasons; because they need something, because they want something, they may be looking to make their job easier, they may be looking to improve their profitability or increase revenue or maybe they feel a need to improve their personal image or their company image.

Win Tip
What is your customer buying today?

Whatever the case, you should be in a position to capitalize on their wants or needs. From your customer's perspective, when they decide to buy something, it would be wonderful if all the competitive sales people immediately came knocking on their door. Unfortunately that doesn't happen and the customer must find out where they can buy whatever it is they are looking for.

Your first task, when you find out your customer is getting ready to buy something, is to find out what they want or need to buy. Although there are a variety of ways for you to find out what your customer wants or needs, the best way is simply for you to ask them.

This is where it gets interesting because waiting for them to make a decision to buy something may not be the best time to ask them what they want to buy. Be proactive and find out what your customer would buy if they were in a buying mode now. When you know exactly what your customer wants or needs to buy, you have an advantage over your competition even though your customer might not be buying it today.

Knowing what your customer wants to buy early in the campaign allows you more time to plan your strategy. The results from a planned strategy are much better then the results from a selling campaign with no strategy at all.

Your customer base is very important because it is this base of people or companies that your future depends upon. You need to build a strong, large base or you will not survive in sales. A good customer base is like a strong foundation and if you put in the effort needed today; you will be continually successful as the years pass.

PROJECTS & BACKLOG

Once you are well on your way to obtaining a rewarding customer base you must then build a strategy for selling to them. A good customer base is only the first step. Now you must work within this customer base to uncover projects. Let's look at our automobile sales people again, the Sales Leader in particular.

While taking those trips out to the farms he generated many new names for his customer base. Even though a farmer may not buy from him this month, it doesn't mean he won't buy from him some day. It warrants his name being incorporated into the sales persons' customer base. Let's say that one of the farmers he visited was not in the market today but said he would be interested next year.

This now becomes a project. Even though the sale won't happen for a year, it will happen one day. Our sales person marks down that the farmer will buy in one year. Now the sales campaign will start. We will talk more about this in a later chapter but basically the sales person will try to position himself at the top of the farmers' mind so when he is ready to buy a vehicle, the farmer will think of this sales person first.

It is up to the sales person to generate more projects. If you are an automobile sales person, you want to have a large amount of projects every month. If you are selling airplanes you would have a much smaller project list but the dollar value of each project would be many times greater. You need to have projects to work on or you will be out of business. Every person who works for a living has projects to work on and so do you.

It is amazing how many sales people don't think this way. They think the business will just come knocking on their door. My comment to that is they better wake up because sales are passing them by.

Once you have generated your list of projects, this becomes your backlog. As long as your backlog is strong your sales will probably be strong as well. Let's say you have a copy of your project list in your hand. On that list are ten projects for next month, nine for the month after and twelve for the month after that. Also on that list are 2 projects for the fourth month. You can now say the next three months should be quite good for sales but the fourth month will be disastrous unless you can find more projects. It works as a guidance system for your sales career.

Those of you who thought this was going to be easy better review your thinking. Selling is not a place for everyone and it is certainly not a last avenue for putting your life back together. A few years ago I heard one gentleman say his life was a mess and he couldn't keep a job so he was going into sales because it was easy. I'm sure he has had a rude awakening by now.

Win Tip
Learn strategies and tactics.

If you don't have a project list to work from you won't be very successful in sales. You must have a project list and you need individual game plans to be implemented for each project. Why take chances at being average when you can do the work, take no chances and be very successful? The sales profession is not a place for loafers and people who are not dedicated and motivated. The tone of this book is built around your desire to succeed and that is the message I want you to walk away with.

There are many ways to track your projects and many reasons to track them as well. You should know what is active and what is hot. You should know what business is coming in next week, next month, next quarter and even for the rest of the year. You must know what your chances are on these projects as well. You could have ten projects in your list and not win any of them. You could also have two projects on your list and be victorious on both occasions. The difference is spinning your wheels and wasting time, or focusing on projects you can win.

Having a project list enables you to better understand where you are with each project. You can be with the customer when it counts instead of at the last minute, or you could uncover a potential problem area soon enough to repair instead of at the last minute.

The more qualified projects you have on your list the more successful you can be. This project list, which we call a backlog, is your strategic sales plan. The bigger the backlog, the more you will win. The more projects you win, the more money you will make.

Many sales people think closing the sale is the toughest part of selling. Closing the sale is easy if you have a large backlog and work your projects in a timely fashion. Closing a sale becomes routine.

COVER YOUR TERRITORY

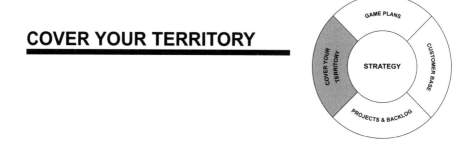

No matter what type of territory you are responsible for, it is up to you to get the most out of it. You could have a geographic territory, a vertical territory or you might even have a territory consisting of a handful of major accounts. No matter what type of territory you cover, that territory is your backyard. Don't let your competitors play in it.

Covering your territory is one of the most complex steps in the sales cycle. So complex, in fact, most average sales people fall flat on their faces when it comes to covering their territory. Sales Leaders implement this function with great success.

The first thing you must do when you receive your territory is find out who lives in it. Usually the downfall of many sales people comes when they start with a new company and they receive their territory list. Nine times out of ten, this list is out of date and inaccurate. You must get out there yourself and identify your new territory.

Here are some of the steps that you need to complete when taking over a new territory. First get the list from management. Next, go out in the territory and get familiar with it. Visit the people on the list. Get a feeling for how much of the list is accurate. After that, dive into your territory and add more names to the list.

Many years ago I moved into a new sales industry and received a territory list that was divided into A, B and C accounts according to the amount of business they brought in. There were more A accounts than there were B and C together. Needless to say, I was quite pleased – at least until I investigated my new territory a little deeper.

I found no A accounts as far as incoming business volumes. There were however, many potential A accounts. This was also the same for B and C accounts. All the three sizes of accounts resided in one city. I also received a geographic territory list for a large area many miles from the city in which I lived. On that list, there were twenty-seven accounts identified.

I was not content with the territory list at all. I decided to go into the territory and make my own list. At least in my mind, that would be more accurate.

A few years later I left that company because of an external promotion. In my tenure I increased sales by 1700%. But that wasn't all. I identified and sold over sixty new projects to customers who were not on my original territory list. On my last day of work for that company I was very proud to hand over an accurate and current territory list.

The point I want you to get out of this is you need to know everything that is going on in your territory. How do you expect to be successful if you don't have a good feeling about your own customer base? There are sales people who lose sale after sale in their territory and they don't even know it. You must go out there and identify every customer in your territory in order to succeed.

Let me give you a comparison of a territory well covered. If you identify each and every customer and build relationships with all of them while at the same time keeping the competition out, that is like buying almost all the tickets in a lottery. You won't win all the time but you will win most of the time.

This is much better that the sales person who doesn't know much about their territory, which seems to be dominated by their competition. That compares to buying one ticket in a lottery – your chances are not very good.

Go out and build a proper territory list. What you received from the company has probably come from a salesperson that either quit or was fired. Every Sales Leader builds his or her own territory list.

You should know every customer and the potential dates of all their future purchases. You must also know everything about your competition. They can be unpredictable. Finally, get into your territory and stay there. Only then will you have a chance at becoming a Sales Leader.

ELRUDE

Elrude Noclue has a geographic territory near the city in which he works. This territory is not very large but he needs to drive about an hour before he gets to it.

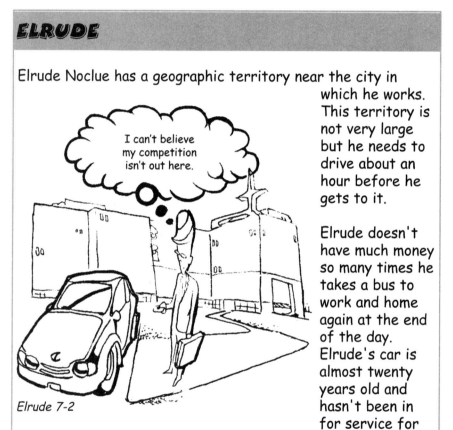

Elrude 7-2

Elrude doesn't have much money so many times he takes a bus to work and home again at the end of the day. Elrude's car is almost twenty years old and hasn't been in for service for the last five years. Elrude proclaims he is so busy at work doing stuff and things that he never has time to take it in for service.

The time has come for Elrude to venture out in the country and spend a couple of days in his territory. His boss told him there are two businesses in his territory in the market for Elrude's product.

The amazing thing we find out about Elrude at this moment is that he actually has a strategy. The problem is that Elrude's strategy is about finding a way to get out of making the trip into his territory.

Elrude hates cold calling, he despises driving, especially in his heap of junk. He does not like being told what to do by his boss and he will miss his night out with the boys. Elrude's short-term thinking has gotten him into a major situation.

Jack Coleman works for a different company and has the same territory as Elrude. He has been making trips there since the territory became his and has built a tight relationship with both companies that are in the market for new products.

Ultimately, Jack wins again and Elrude is left complaining to his boss that he should never have gone out there in the first place. It was a waste of time and money. Elrude explained to his boss the territory was never going to generate any business and he would be happy to give it up and concentrate more on the stuff and things he is doing in the city.

Summary

Take the time to plan before you make your moves. You must own a strategy or you will become easy prey for your competition. Build a game plan, set goals, find out who and where your customers are, build a list of future projects and work your territory.

Strategy is what sales people must use every day. When two sales people are chasing the same opportunity, it is quite easy to distinguish between the one who uses a strategy and the one who doesn't. A clearly laid out strategy will put you in control and allow you to prioritize and complete your tasks.

Win Process: Strategy

☑ Game Plan   What you are going to do next

☑ Strategy   An overall plan

☑ Customer Base   Where you business will come from

☑ Project   A sales opportunity

☑ Backlog   A list of projects

☑ Territory   Your business backyard

☑ Thought   Put it into every plan

☑ Proactive   Always plan ahead

Win Notes: My Strategy

Use this page to assess your sales strategy. What are your strengths? Where do you need to improve?

8   **Customer Relationships**

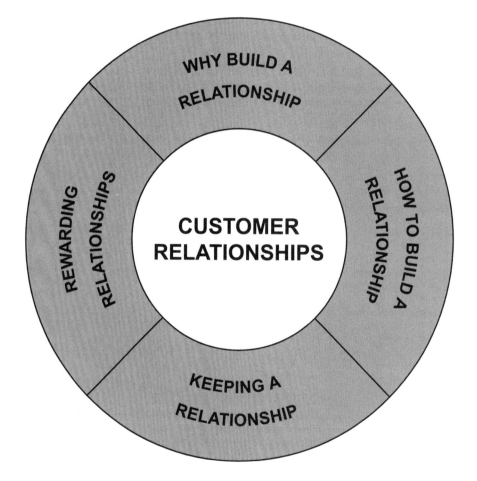

Customer Relationships   8

Sales Leaders thrive on building great customer relationships. Have you ever heard a sales person say that he or she won a sale on the golf course? What they really mean is they built a relationship with a customer to the extent where they became more than just business associates. They actually became friends with their customer. When this happens for you an entire new world is accessed. You now have the advantage.

Customer relationships are one of the most important aspects of the sales process. Although great customer relationships will not win every sale for you, they will improve your chances immensely. In this chapter we are going to learn why we build relationships, how to build relationships and how to keep relationships. We will close this chapter off by making sure we understand the rewards of a relationship and how to keep those rewards coming in.

WHY BUILD A RELATIONSHIP

Why do we spend all that extra time trying to fully understand our customers when all we need to do is sell them whatever it is we are selling? The answer is simple. As time goes by there are more and more sales people selling similar products to yours to the same customers as you. In your customers' eyes, and with very few exceptions, the product you are selling isn't much different than your competitors' product.

When there are many sales people from different companies trying to sell products to a customer and the products are all similar in features, cost, appeal and delivery, then something else has to make the difference. That difference is you.

Let's look at this from the customers' perspective. Say you are buying office furniture for your company. There are six office furniture sales people calling on you and giving you prices for this furniture. You look at all the products these sales people offer and you find something very interesting. All sales people have quoted you similar office furniture with similar guarantees and deliveries. The prices, amazingly enough, are all within ten percent of each other.

You realize there is really no difference between any of the offerings. You would be just as happy with any of the furniture that was quoted to you. So now you can just put everybody's name in a hat and pick one.

Win Tip
Build relationships with decision makers.

What would happen if one of those sales people decided to build a relationship with you? What if one of those sales people showed you that he or she cared enough about you that they went that extra step to make you feel more comfortable in dealing with them than anyone else? What if they mixed in personal data and stepped through the business barrier? What if they became a small part of your personal life and you became part of their personal life as well? What if you now felt closer to that sales person than any of the others? Everything else being equal, you would probably give them the order.

If you don't build relationships with your customers, every sale you chase will end up the same way – hoping your name gets picked out of the hat. Let's see what your odds are of winning if every sale ends up with a decision being made by picking names out of a hat.

If there is only one other competitor, then you have a fifty percent chance of winning. If there are three competitors and yourself, you have a twenty-five percent chance of winning. Usually many hours of work go into a sales campaign; shouldn't you have some control in the decision? Why would you do all that work if you are not increasing your chances of winning?

Now, let's take this a bit deeper. What do you think your chances are if there are three competitors and yourself and one of these competitors has a good relationship with the customer? Your chances now drop to almost zero. It becomes a no-win situation for you. I have witnessed many sales people lose sale after sale for this very reason. The sales person knows and understands his own product and all his competitors' products, but he has not developed a relationship with the customer. He doesn't understand how important customer relationships really are to sales success.

Let's define a customer relationship. It is a bond of friendship, trust and loyalty that is formed between a sales person and a customer that sets up a commitment where both parties succeed in attaining their goals while helping the other attain theirs. Usually the goal of the sales person is very different than the goal of the decision maker but both parties' realize they must help each other in order to help themselves.

ELRUDE

Elrude Noclue and Jack Coleman are at it again. Jack has been building a relationship with a customer for almost three years, even though this particular customer was not in the market to buy anything. Elrude has been busy doing stuff and things and trying hard to win his first sale.

Jack realizes that building customer relationships is very important, especially when the customer is not in buying mode. It allows for a potential relationship to develop. He knows it is easier to build credibility with a customer when they are not buying anything. The customer has time to see Jack and there is no time or other pressures – this relationship will grow and develop naturally.

Elrude operates from day to day and feels that building a customer relationship at a time when the customer is not buying anything is a pure waste of his time. Being reactive, Elrude thrives on last minute sales efforts.

This particular customer has finally decided it is time to replace his old product with something new. He has his budget approved and the funds have been allocated to this project.

Now he has to go out and find this new product.

The customer feels he can save additional money if he does not ask for competitive bids. He already knows that Jack Coleman has a powerful product to replace his old equipment. But he still feels the need to interview one other supplier before he can award this order to Jack.

Elrude 8-1

The customer calls Elrude's company and asks for the sales person who looks after his account. The hot lead is given to Elrude and the sales process begins.

Elrude calls the customer and sets up a meeting for the next day. Elrude arrives twenty minutes late because he missed a bus connection. Since he didn't call to say he would be late, his customer went off to do something else after ten minutes of waiting.

A secretary finds the customer and he returns for his meeting with Elrude. The meeting starts with Elrude presenting his product. He never apologized for being late. He never asked any questions about what the customer wanted. There was no small talk. No attempt at building a last minute relationship. Elrude went right to presentation mode and talked and talked and talked. This went on for fifteen minutes and ended only because the customer terminated the meeting.

The customer decided there was no comparison between

Elrude and Jack. He felt foolish for even doubting his relationship with Jack and his company. He immediately called Jack and awarded him the order.

Elrude reported his position to his boss. He told him the customer was an idiot. The customer called Elrude to schedule a meeting about his product, and in the middle of the presentation asked Elrude to stop and leave; another waste of time in Elrude's eyes.

Several days later when Jack was having lunch with his customer, the story was recited to Jack about the meeting with Elrude. Both parties laughed and Jack never said a word about his previous encounters with Elrude. That would be unethical, he thought.

Jack knew it was only a matter of time before he was promoted to manager and he looked forward to the years ahead. Maybe he could hire Elrude and teach him how to sell. Now that would be a great challenge.

Building a customer relationship doesn't just happen. You must work at it. You should know who to build these relationships with. You can ruin a good sales campaign by building a relationship with the wrong person. Always build your relationships with people who can make buying decisions or influence buying decisions. There is no value in building a relationship with a truck driver in a freight company when you are trying to sell office supplies to the company secretary.

HOW TO BUILD A RELATIONSHIP

This is one of the most important pieces you must learn in your drive to becoming a Sales Leader. Some sales people think they know how to build a good customer relationship but in all honesty, they really don't. Sales Leaders are able to adjust their personality to allow them to build relationships with any customer.

I have talked and worked with many sales people in my career and I have always found it amazing to hear some say customer relationships are not important. I heard it twenty years ago and I still hear it today. It makes me wonder what sales people are thinking when they make comments like that. I believe it proves that sometimes sales are lost and the sales person doesn't know why. The problem compounds for them as well because if they never know why they lost a sale then they will make the same mistake again on the next campaign.

I mentioned earlier about having a flexible personality if you are trying to build customer relationships. This is very important because every customer is different. You must have the ability to mold and change your personality and behavior to fit your customers'.

Win Tip

A strong customer relationship is built on trust.

If you are not well organized or late with your follow-up calls then you must make changes in yourself if you want to build a good relationship with a customer who is attentive, well organized and prompt. Sales Leaders are able to adjust their personalities quickly.

In order to be flexible with your personality, you should approach your customer for the first time with caution. Don't commit yourself in any direction until you understand your customer's personality. Then you can adjust your personality to fit their style.

I have heard sales people say things like this lost a sales campaign: 'We had a good product fit but the customer and I just couldn't see eye to eye.' 'He always wanted something different than what I was giving him. Even though I could always give him what he wanted, I could never figure him out.' 'There always seemed to be tension between us.' 'I guess he just doesn't like sales people.'

Somebody should tell these sales people they lost the job to another sales person – one who was better at building customer relationships. Who did the sales people think they lost the sale to anyway, a doctor or a lawyer? No, another sales person outsold them.

In order to build relationships with all your customers you must be a nice person. Show an interest in your customer both personally and professionally. The relationship must be a two-way street. You will need to know as much or more about them as they know about you. Show interest in their reasons for potentially buying your product. Listen and understand what they are trying to do.

Win Tip

It is rewarding to be considered trustworthy.

Another task to complete when developing a good relationship is to build trust in one another. Once the trust level is established, the relationship should be fairly well in place. You must build trust in the customer as the customer builds trust in you.

KEEPING A RELATIONSHIP

Once you build a strong relationship with your customer, find ways to keep the relationship alive. You will get most of your sales from existing accounts over time. If a good relationship with your customer will help you win the original sale, think how important it will be to keep the relationship going if most of your sales derive from existing accounts.

You must keep a relationship going with your customer to stay credible in their eyes. Whatever you did to win the original order must be maintained if you want all subsequent orders. It doesn't matter what you are selling, relationships are important. If you are a computer sales person and you sold a computer package to a customer, chances are that customer will buy all their add-ons from you and when it is time to buy a new computer, they will automatically come to you as well – if they like and trust you.

A few years ago my wife and I bought new mountain bikes so we could ride the bike trails of this great city we live in. We bought the bikes from the sales person we liked, who happened to be the owner of a bike store. He used great relationship selling to convince us to buy from him. The other bike stores had similar bikes at similar prices, but we wanted to deal with this person because he made us feel comfortable. He asked questions about where and how often we would ride our bikes. He gave us advice on which trails were more scenic or less congested than others. He showed us he cared about our riding enjoyment.

We owned the bikes only two months when they were stolen from our garage. They had to be replaced so we went back to the same sales person and bought two more. We never looked anywhere else. We also bought more expensive bikes the second time. The sales person treated us well the first time. He treated us even better the second time.

Over the next few years we purchased a variety of items from the same sales person – cycle gloves, helmets, saddlebags and cycle pants. Again, we never looked anywhere else. A year after that, our first son was born and we went back to purchase a trailer that fastened to the back of our bikes so we could still ride the trails and take our son with us.

This sales person first won our business by putting together a selling strategy aimed at winning business. He was nice to us right from the start. He addressed my wife as much as he addressed me because he knew both of us were making the decision together. He asked us many questions and made us feel comfortable dealing with him.

We had just been to a couple of other bike shops and the sales people there immediately tried to sell us a bike from their store. The sales person we purchased our bikes from didn't try to sell us a bike from his store. He sold us the bikes we were looking for and it just happened he had a couple in his store. The difference is he found out, through detailed questioning, exactly what we wanted, then he sold it to us. He built a relationship with us first, and then he sold us our bikes. His competition never tried to build a relationship at all.

We continue to buy products from this sales person, even though he has moved his bike store to a different part of the city farther from our house. We continue to buy from him because he still makes us feel comfortable and always remembers our names, even if we don't visit his store for a year.

Two other tasks you must do to maintain a good customer relationship are: continue to show as much interest in your customers as you did originally, and continue to be reliable. Treat every interaction with them like it is their first purchase. The first sale to a customer is usually the hardest, don't give up and walk away from all the additional sales that will come later.

REWARDING RELATIONSHIPS

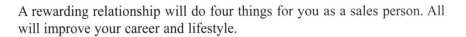

A rewarding relationship will do four things for you as a sales person. All will improve your career and lifestyle.

Each time you build a rewarding relationship you are meeting a brand new friend. Many times these new friendships are for life. Customers are people just like us and it is amazing how similar everyone can be.

Rewarding relationships will also generate more repeat sales for you in your career. Your success in sales will certainly be much higher then sales people who do not build good customer relationships. It's been my experience and the experience of other Sales Leaders I know that repeat business is worth approximately ten times the original sale, in a transaction-based selling environment. In a recurring revenue environment, that number is even higher. Which sales person would you rather be?

Win Tip

Have you ever became friends with a customer?

A greater number of sales may not be your only ticket to success. It has been proven over and over the best sales people are the first to get promoted to management and even further up the ladder to senior management. Many good sales people even become presidents of companies. Rewarding relationships will enhance your career and help you generate more success for yourself.

Finally, you will become more marketable within your own company and outside your organization as well. The more companies that want you, the better off you are. The stakes get raised and you win with more money where it counts – in your pocket.

Summary

Rewarding relationships are something to cherish. You can dedicate your career to building rewarding relationships and the payoff is immense. Maintain the ability to build customer relationships and develop a passion for selling by keeping these relationships intact and running smoothly for many, many years.

A strong **Customer Relationship** will put you in a favorable position in most sales campaigns. When you build relationships with your customer base you are taking control of your success. When all else is equal, the sales person with the best customer relationship will win.

Win Process:
Customer Relationships

☑ Friend   Result of a strong customer relationship

☑ People   They are all different

☑ Influence   Possible decision converter

☑ Decision   The verdict

☑ Successful   When you continually win

☑ Relationship   A strong bond

☑ Rewarding   When all players win

☑ Loyalty   Offering commitment

Win Notes: My Customer Relationships

Use this page to assess your existing customer relationships. What are your strengths? Where do you need to improve?

9   Put in the Hours

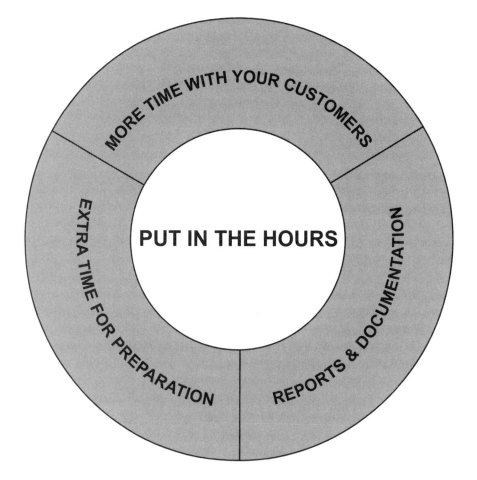

Put in the Hours 9

People who put in extra hours at work usually do it because they can make additional money for working overtime. The more overtime sales people work will help them make more money as well, but it doesn't come in the form of extra wages. It appears as a bonus or commission or even a promotion. Sales people who put in extra effort will usually make it farther up the corporate ladder than sales people who don't.

There is no rule that says you have to work extra time but experience will tell you the more hours you work, the faster you will get to the top.

Early in my sales career I worked many extra hours. I did that because I was on a one hundred percent commission compensation plan and that was how much time I had to work just to make enough money to pay my bills.

Moving forward in my career, I still worked many extra hours. This time the reason was slightly different. First, I increased my sales and made more money in the form of commission payments. Secondly though, I put in more hours so I could cover all my accounts properly and ensure all my reports and documents were completed on time. I also like to take time to prepare.

Now that I'm in management, I work even more hours than I did before – typically between sixty and seventy a week. It's tough to get everything done in a normal workday because there are many distractions and interruptions. Managers put in more hours trying to find ways to maximize sales while cutting costs. The more effort you can put in to your profession will help make you more successful in the end.

Sales Leaders are very efficient and usually break up their day into grouped tasks. They start early, usually in the office by 7:00. This gives them an hour or more to prepare their day and complete unfinished paperwork. They will spend from 8:30 to 4:30 in front of as many customers as possible. (What better way to find out where the opportunities are?) Then back in the office by 5:00 to finish making notes from the appointments they have just completed. Sometimes they go home at 5:00 but may spend an hour or two in the evening preparing for the next day.

On the other hand, I have seen many sales people have less productive days. They arrive at the office half an hour late and spend the next hour talking about sports, what they did last night, reading the paper, drinking coffee and simply annoying other people.

Win Tip

The harder you work, the faster you will get to the top.

For the rest of the morning they hang around their desk shuffling paper from one pile to another and back again telling their co-workers how tough the market is right now. They leave for lunch at 11:30 and return around 1:30 to sit at their desk for another hour talking to friends on the telephone. At about 2:30 they leave the office to attend appointments, but not before telling everyone in the office how busy their day has been and they have three meetings before they go home. But we're never quite sure where these meetings are… They return the next day to start the process all over again. Sound familiar? Have you seen sales people act this way? Where are they now? Where will they be in six months?

MORE TIME WITH YOUR CUSTOMERS

I strongly believe in two points with regard to customers. I believe in customer entertainment after hours. I also believe in making that one extra sales call every day. Let's talk about the one extra sales call first. This is one of the hardest commitments for anyone to make. Its 4:00 and you are just finishing a busy day. You want to go home. You have done enough work for today.

Sales people who feel like this typically generate average or below average sales results. Maybe a few years ago these average results were satisfactory for many companies but in today's market where margins are smaller, total sales revenue becomes quite important. Therefore more sales people are putting in extra effort – just to keep up. This means making one extra sales call – just to be average.

We will discuss your competition in the next chapter but I will mention now that you must contribute with a strong effort if you plan on winning more than them. There are many more educated sales people on the street today than there were a few years ago. That relates to a longer and more in-depth selling process.

Most sales people today have eased off trying to ram products down the customer's throat. The repeat business from this type of selling style is not very good. Sales people today are working smarter and working harder. By working smarter, they are trying to build strategies and use acceptable tactics that will enable them to keep existing customers, as well as win new customers. By working harder, sales people today are creating a better position for themselves within their company by generating more revenue than what is expected. I guess the question here is this: How does working harder generate more revenue?

Win Tip

Make that one extra sales call every day.

The answer is very simple. Take your total sales for a given day, week or month and divide that number by the actual hours you worked over that time and you will get a number representing the revenue you generate for your company on an hourly basis – but only if you win the business. If not, all you effort was for naught. If you increase the amount of hours you work in a week you should increase the total revenue you generate for your company. I say 'should' here because, as we see elsewhere in this book, there are many ways for sale people to undermine their own efforts.

If you think you have one whole year to achieve or exceed your quota – think again. You actually have only about 45 weeks, or 10 months to make your numbers. This figure drops as the amount of time you are away from your selling job increases (internal meetings, additional days off, etc.). It also drops with every sale you fail to win.

Here is an example. Let's assume your annual sales quota is $1 million, and your typical workday is 7.5 hours long.

Activity	Hours	Days	Weeks
Worktime	1950	260	52
Less Statutory Holidays	<82.5>	<11>	<2>
Sub-total	1867.5	249	50
Less Vacation	<112.5>	<15>	<3>
Sub-total	1755	234	47
Less Training Time	<37.5>	<5>	<1>
Sub-total	1717.5	229	46
Less Sales Team Meetings	<45>	<6>	<1>
Total	1672.5	223	45
Impact on $1 million Quota	**$598/hr**	**$4,484/day**	**$22,421/wk**

If you can make or exceed your quota within your regular workday, then good on you. But by far the vast majority of sales people need to put in extra time in order to just make the numbers.

Who benefits by putting in this extra work? The answer is everyone except your competition. Your customer benefits because they see more of you and a comfort level is reached where your availability becomes important to them – remember our earlier discussions on customer relationships. Your company benefits because you are generating more revenue for them and you benefit by earning a bonus or more commission for that additional time you commit to your sales success.

We are all in charge of our own destinies and the more you put into your work, the more you will get out of it. Put more effort than your competition into covering your customer base or you will only be average, at best. Average is not good enough anymore. As a matter of fact, next year you will need to be better then you are this year if you plan on having a successful career in sales.

In most organizations, sales quotas rise each year. When I started selling in the late 1970's my quota was $100,000. By the mid 1990's my annual quota was over $4 million. That is a 4000% increase in almost twenty years. Although I changed industries, numbers like that are very common throughout the sales profession. Companies always want more from you this year than they got from you last year.

That philosophy hasn't changed in years and I can't really see it changing anytime in the near future. Companies will always need, want and expect more than they are getting from their reps today. It is up to you to give this to them. One thing is for sure, if you don't, they will find someone else out there who will.

The harder you work, the faster you will get to the top. I know many people will say you don't have to work harder, you just have to work smarter. With all due respect, I believe we need to do both. By working smarter and not harder you are completing only half your job. That's not good enough anymore.

Win Tip
Sales people are hired to win.

You will hear sales people say they can't mix business and pleasure. These people have not yet adapted the right personality for their job. So what type of personality do you need to be successful in this field? A personality that is flexible certainly comes to my mind. Another important trait is happiness and a third is stability. If you design your personality around these traits and routinely practice adapting it to your customers, you will become more successful.

Two things happen when you entertain customers after hours. First, you remove them from their work environment (and all the accompanying distractions) and second, you move them into a relaxing environment where you gain more control. You are probably wondering why a customer is not in control when he or she is not in their office. The answer is simple. When you entertain customers you are paying the bill. This puts you in control.

REPORTS & DOCUMENTATION

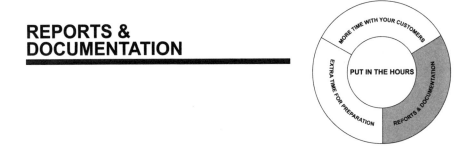

With any sales position there is always paperwork that needs to be completed. During the last ten years of my selling career I was required to complete about two hours a day of paperwork – sales call reports, letters, e-mails, proposals, quotes, sales plans, marketing plans, project reports, as well as general notes. Whatever paperwork you are working on, make sure it is completed to the best of your ability. Many sales people get promoted into management not just because they were great at selling, but also because they were magnificent at completing paperwork on time or ahead of schedule.

Today, sales managers are more demanding and their expectations are very high when it comes to reporting. All of these reports are needed for constant budgeting and fine tuning of the business sales plan. Reporting and documenting sometimes seem useless to many sales people but there is value associated with it and if you can master the task of preparing this paperwork during non-selling hours, you are ahead of your competition.

You must have a desire to succeed. You must work smart as well as hard. First you work smart to define all your tasks and put them in the proper order to be completed. By working smart, you don't just fill an eight hour day with tasks. You fill a ten hour day or a twelve hour day of however many extra hours you need to work. Then you work hard by completing all the tasks you have assigned to yourself. This is the formula for sales success.

I am sure most of you have ridden in a taxi and are familiar with their payment method. The small mileage and time counter on the dash just keeps clicking until you reach your destination. By the time you reach your destination, you pay whatever the little machine says you owe. Imagine you are in a taxi and driving across town when all of a sudden the taxi driver turns around and says, "I am going to let you out here because it is 4:45 and it is time for me to quit driving for the day. I have to tally up all my paperwork and get it back to the office before I leave for home at 5:00." Certainly that would leave you in a bind. Keep this in mind each time you decide to complete your paperwork during business hours, when you should be in front of your customers.

EXTRA TIME FOR PREPARATION

You have decided to spend the entire business day in front of customers and you have also decided to complete all of your paperwork either very early in the morning or later at night while you are at home. Qualifying this extra effort is the next step.

You are now spending more time in front of your customers, but are you prepared? Increased sales calls require more planning. How can we handle this planning? Having one qualified sales call in a day is better than having five unqualified calls. That is why you must plan who you are going to see, why you are going to see them and what you plan to accomplish while you are there. Taking your customer out for lunch because you are hungry does not constitute a qualified sales call. You must make a plan.

Now that you have a full day of meetings, when do you think you will find the time to plan your strategy for these meetings? You could plan at home in the evening or maybe early in the morning before you go to the office. Mix it in with the paperwork you are required to complete as well.

Take a positive attitude to this and always remember that every extra hour you work will either directly or indirectly put more money in your pocket. If you plan on working only eight hours a day you will probably struggle to keep up. There are more sales people today then ever before. These sales people also have a higher level of education – many of them have business degrees. They have learned flexibility and creative thinking. It won't be too long and they will be outselling you. If this happens, you have a choice: either watch your sales dwindle away, or control your own destiny and stop all of this from happening by winning your campaigns.

Take extra time to plan your sales calls so you will be at your best. Develop and use an action plan. Practice what you plan to say to your customers. Ask yourself the questions you plan on asking them. Make sure you are set up to be in control during these calls. If you don't feel comfortable, practice again. Take all the extra time you need. Get it right before you get in front of your customer.

ELRUDE

Elrude Noclue works enough hours in a day to get by. He usually struggles to spend forty hours a week doing his job. One day he stumbled across a mammoth project that could help him become the great sales person he so desired to be.

He could make history if he won this sale. In his unorthodox way he managed to get in front of the customer. He asked questions and actually listened to the answers. He kept notes and designed his presentation. He thought he was working hard staying within the guidelines of a forty hour week.

This project engrossed him. He had no time for anything else. When it came time for him to step up and deliver his presentation, he realized he had forgotten to prepare. There had not been enough time in his day to plan or prepare for his presentation. No problem, he had winged it before and he will just wing it again.

It took Elrude almost two hours to say everything he needed to say in order to complete his presentation. He realized part way through the presentation that he was not in control and was being compared to his competition. He began to feel uncomfortable. Twinges in his stomach told him he was heading for another loss. He hated that feeling.

When Jack Coleman completed his presentation to the same customer he was completely prepared. He had executed a number of dry runs and planned for every possible excuse and interruption.

Jack chased this project for many weeks. He maintained his habit of placing himself in front of his customers during the day while working evenings preparing and planning for this presentation.

Elrude 9-1

All his hard work paid off and again he was successful. He was not surprised because he had planned on winning. He put in the extra hours planning and preparing and was rewarded for his efforts.

Elrude Noclue was not surprised when he heard he had lost again. He knew he needed to plan but he had never done that before and he was too scared to try. He made himself feel better by saying this project was too large for his company anyway.

Summary

Put in the extra hours and spend more time with your customers. Business hours are selling hours. Make sure your paperwork is up to date, and do it during non-selling hours. Your success depends on your effort. And your effort must be directed toward your success. If you don't distance yourself from your competition, you will be average, and your name goes into the hat.

When you **Put in the Hours** each day you are giving yourself a better chance of winning more work. Most of your competition will not put in any more hours than they need to.

Win Process:
Put in the Hours

☑ Overtime   Foundation for more wins

☑ Commission   Your reward for winning

☑ Extra   Type of work you should do each day

☑ Average   Nothing you want to be

☑ After Hours   Time for doing paperwork

☑ Paperwork   What you do after hours

☑ Reports   Documenting your efforts

☑ Time   Take some and make one more call

Win Notes: My Hours

Use this page to assess your work schedule. What are your strengths? Where do you need to improve?

10 Know Your Competition

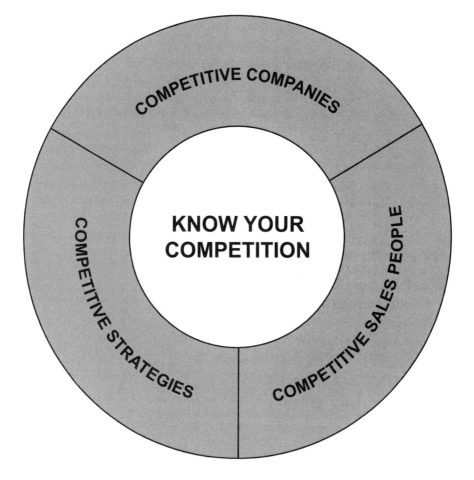

Know Your Competition 10

You may know your products very well, understand your customer's needs and be able to present your products effectively, but if you don't know your competition, you are at a disadvantage and could lose the sale. If any of your competitors are Sales Leaders, you can be sure they know about you.

In this chapter we will gain an understanding about what companies do to outsmart their competition. Next, we will learn about competitive sales people and understand how they can defeat you in a sales campaign. Finally, we will talk about competitive strategies and how to implement ones that will help you win more often. You will also learn about making the transition from being taken advantage of by your competition to gaining and keeping competitive advantage.

COMPETITIVE COMPANIES

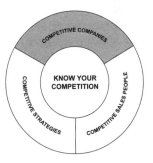

Companies will try almost anything to win sales. In the past, some companies utilized a successful advertising technique that revolutionized the sales world. It was based on a very simple principle and is still used today.

All these advertisements did was drive home the fact their product was the easiest to use, best looking, longest lasting, most durable, offered the best warranty, had the fastest delivery and was the lowest price.

Many companies were not exactly sure what their customers wanted so they promoted an image of being the supplier of everything. Customers would see these advertisements and place orders accordingly. Competitive selling had reached a new level. Tell your customer about everything you offer and they will be sure to pick something. This was quite effective for many years until the competition started selling in the same fashion. Full-scale changes would take place again.

Let's say your product is easier to use and priced lower than a similar product from your competitors. Obviously your company must advertise this fact to generate the level of success it requires. Therefore, your product could be better than your competition's product but if your competitor builds a perception of theirs being better, they win and you lose unless you provide the proper information to the customer.

Win Tip

Don´t let your competition steal your business.

When I was selling insurance many years ago, brokers were associated with particular underwriters. My company changed things up a bit by advertising that we brokered for many different insurance underwriters. The image my company promoted was, no matter the customer's needs, we had a product suited just for them. The benefit for the customers was choice.

The brokered approach was not previously available to the people of my hometown and it became quite a hit. Most other insurance companies offered only a handful of different types of insurance plans while my company offered many different plans. We generated extra business because of this novel approach and became one of the most successful insurance companies in the area.

It became the customer's perception that the company I worked for offered a greater choice of insurance plans with prices that fit their needs better. This was true. It also became the customer's perception that because we had so many plans to choose from, they were getting the best plan on the market for the money they were spending. This was true as well.

Now let's look at an amazing statistic. Almost 90% of all the insurance plans my company sold were from one underwriter. Almost 90% of the customers bought the same plan. If we brokered for just this one underwriter we would not have been as successful. Choice was our differentiator. We became more successful when my company decided to outsmart the competition.

Companies are in business to make money. A great company helps its sales force succeed. It is then up to the sales people to capitalize on whatever strategic plan the company puts in place.

There are other ways in which your company can get ahead of the competition. One common way is teach the sales people about the competition's products. This is a good strategy because you learn the strong points and benefits as well as the weak areas that add little value.

Win Tip
Winning is easier when you know about your competition.

However, there are two problems with this type of analysis. First, most companies are doing this so if your company isn't teaching you about competitive products you will end up behind and find it hard to catch up. You may not realize your full sales potential if your company isn't giving you all the sales tools that your competitors are providing for their sales people.

The other problem associated with this strategy is volume. Because there are so many new products entering the marketplace every day, you could spend all your time learning your competitor's product and no time actually selling.

Always remember that you have to stay focused on your customer and never look back at your competition. If you were running in a very important race in which you were leading, would you keep looking back behind you? If you did that, you might trip and fall. You might lose your focus if you became preoccupied with the size of your lead. This is exactly what your competition wants. They can make you lose your focus quite easily.

If I was right behind you in a foot race and I yelled to you I was gaining and was going to pass you soon, what would you do? The experienced people would bear down, not lose focus and would probably still win. The inexperienced people would lose focus and look back to see where I was. I would be starting to pass them about now.

Learn as much as you can about the companies you compete against.

Understand your competition and leverage this information in your sales campaign. There should now be one less reason for you to lose.

COMPETITIVE SALES PEOPLE

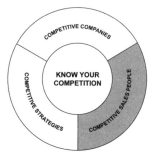

There is one type of competitive sales person that will give even the best sales people a problem. This is a sales person who will lie to get the sale. These people will not be successful in the long term and usually they will not stay in the sales game very long. Don't ever lie to a customer. It will cost you your career. You must be ethical. Lying to your customer will cost your company a serious amount of revenue in future lost sales. Lying to your customer will damage your credibility forever.

In your sales career you will meet many different types of sales people. These people are not your enemy. They may think they are your enemy and they might even treat you like their enemy. But think about this: all competitive sales people (internal and external) can help you win more sales than you could ever imagine. Earlier in this chapter we discussed how your company can create a perception with customers that they are the best. Through this perception they increase sales and gain a larger portion of market share. You can create the same type of perception with your competition.

Let's say your company hires a new sales person. Your boss introduces you to Bob, the new employee. During the introduction your boss mentions that you are a successful sales person. From that day on Bob believes you are a successful sales person simply because your boss told him you are. Bob will always look at you as a successful sales person as long as your boss continues to do the same.

Now let's say you get to know a few of your competitors in the industry.

You are introduced to Ken, who happens to be a very successful sales person working with your competition. You may think he is successful only because someone told you he was. What will happen when you run into him in a competitive situation? He may already have you beat because he knows you think he is successful. More importantly, he knows that you are not. He has outsold you with perception. Don't let these people fool you for a minute. They are no better then you and in most cases, they are not as good as you. They just know how to play the game better.

This is why you must know as much as you can about your competition. There are no rules when it comes to your competition. In most cases, they will do whatever it takes to win. It is up to you to know who these people are, what they do and where they go. To be victorious in a sales campaign you need to defeat your competition. Shouldn't you know something about them?

Win Tip
Know more about your competition than they know about you.

Maybe you play hockey and you score many goals because you shoot the puck hard and high, making goaltenders cringe and duck. Then one day you play against a goaltender with a very quick glove hand. So fast in fact he stops all your shots. He frustrates you but you just keep shooting harder and higher. He catches every shot you send his way and your team loses. How would you feel if after the game I told you this goaltender couldn't stop anything that was on the ice, and if you kept your shots low you probably would have scored many times?

It all comes down to knowing your competition. You must find out everything you can about them. Your success will arrive when you understand how they sell. All you need to do to win is outsell your competition. Take the time to get to know them. The best way is to ask your customers about them. They will usually tell you what you want to know.

Everyone builds great relationships with some customers. You must find out which customers your competition has built relationships with and put a counter-strategy in place or you won't get any of that customers' business. When you build a good customer relationship with someone, you expect to win some business. When your competition builds a good customer relationship with someone, they expect to win as well. You should find out

where these alliances are and start building your own relationships with those customers.

Elrude Noclue was getting ready for his next selling adventure. He recently heard about a company that was about to make a new purchase. Elrude had exactly what they were looking for so he set out on a path to convince them to buy from him.

Elrude worked hard to finally get a face-to-face meeting with the decision maker. He asked some questions and only partially listened to the answers as his mind wandered, thinking about how he would spend the commission he would earn for winning this deal.

When the meeting was almost over, Elrude asked a question that set the stage for some interesting thought. He asked if his customer had any relationships in place with competing sales people. This was quite advanced questioning, especially from Elrude.

His customer answered yes – Jack Coleman. He said he has known Jack for almost ten years and has purchased many items from Jack over that time. He also told Elrude that Jack was the favorite to win this project because of the relationship in place. Elrude ended the meeting by suggesting to his customer he would try to get to know Jack Coleman to see what makes him tick. His customer agreed, because Jack knows quite a bit about Elrude. Jack even told his customer Elrude would likely call him this week. Elrude was shocked to hear this. He asked his customer what else Jack knew about him and his customer replied he knew Elrude has yet to win any sales. He said Jack knows most things he needs to know to be successful and since Elrude does not have any victories, Jack doesn't worry about him. He concluded by saying Jack still watches Elrude and asks about him occasionally.

Elrude walked out of his customers' office with disbelief

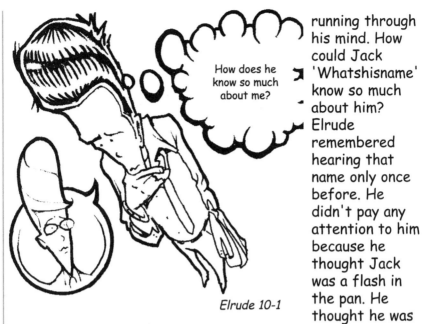

running through his mind. How could Jack 'Whatshisname' know so much about him? Elrude remembered hearing that name only once before. He didn't pay any attention to him because he thought Jack was a flash in the pan. He thought he was some sales person who was around for a couple of sales then left for greener grass somewhere else.

Elrude 10-1

A couple of weeks passed and Elrude received another letter stating he had lost again. He immediately called his customer to ask who won and he wasn't surprised when he heard the name Jack Coleman.

Elrude knew exactly what he had to do. He picked up the phone and made a call.

Equally important is building relationships with your competitors. Knowing and understanding them can give you valuable insight about how they conduct sales campaigns. An easy way to do this is to contact a competitor and ask for a meeting. Once you and your competitor are together, talk about what has made both of you successful. Discuss other sales people you compete against and discuss how to be victorious over them.

Now comes the important part. It's well known that sales people love talking about themselves. Leverage this trait by asking your competitor as many questions about him as you can. Find out how he thinks, what motivates him, his background, his views on the industry, and where he sees himself in the next few years. Listen attentively to his answers. Somewhere in the conversation you will hear something that will be of value to you down the road.

Don't stop here. Work this type of magic with all your competitors. Every sales person has at least one weak point and it is up to you to find it. You must learn to take advantage of your competition because they are trying to take advantage of you. You can win or you can lose, the choice is yours. Certainly, winning is more fun, and more rewarding.

ELRUDE

Elrude Noclue was nervous when he pulled his old car into the parking lot of his favorite restaurant. It had been almost two years since he was here. Being without a victory has drained his finances to the point where this is a luxury he cannot afford.

Today was different though and he knew this was going to be money well spent. For the first time in his life, Elrude Noclue had a plan. His boss told him this would never work and tried hard to talk him out of it. He even told Elrude he would not pay for the lunch. Elrude still forged ahead. He knew what he was doing was right and it would offer him a chance that would affect his life forever. He knew he had nothing to lose and everything to gain.

Elrude scanned the restaurant and no one looked familiar. Suddenly a hand darted into the air and Elrude waved as he made his way to the table near the back.

Jack Coleman stood and shook Elrude's hand with authority. He couldn't believe he was here in person with the 'legend of losing' as he had so often heard about Elrude. Jack told Elrude it was a pleasure to meet him and quickly set the tone of the meeting by telling Elrude of his most recent victories.

The meeting lasted almost two hours and both sales people

Wow, the "legend of losing" in person!

Jack, you're much shorter than I imagined.

enjoyed each other's company. They laughed and talked about the sales campaigns they had chased together. Jack told most of the stories because Elrude never seemed to have enough information to piece a full story together.

Elrude 10-2

The meeting ended and both sales people were on their way to their next appointments. Jack didn't learn anything new about Elrude he didn't already know and was unsure why Elrude requested the meeting. It seemed out of character for Elrude to do this.

Elrude learned two valuable lessons during that meeting. He learned he was far behind when it came to planning. He also learned he had no relationships in place while Jack appeared to have many.

COMPETITIVE STRATEGIES

COMPETITIVE COMPANIES

KNOW YOUR COMPETITION

COMPETITIVE SALES PEOPLE

COMPETITIVE STRATEGIES

It is important to gain control and stay there. A sale is almost impossible to win if you are not in control.

Sales people are responsible for bringing in a company's revenue. Selling is a profession that requires you to think. If you are in this profession because there is nowhere else to go, you will get pummeled by the competition. Sales Leaders will defeat you with ease. They will outsmart you, out-think you, outsell you, and outwork you any day of the week. You must plan, prepare and practice for every sales campaign. Whoever does the best job at this wins the game.

I once knew a sales person who was well educated and had many years of selling experience. His goal was to learn something new every day. This person did not lose very often. He knew more about his territory, his products, his customers and his competition then anyone he competed against. Winning was second nature for him.

He displayed the image of a Sales Leader. He was a great communicator and he listened intently to all his customer's needs. He was a personable, approachable man with many creative ideas. He was not overbearing but he did stand out in a crowd. He had many great attributes that contributed to his success. But it was his skill at developing and executing a strategy, as well as his unique ability to build customer relationships that made him a true Sales Leader.

Win Tip

You can beat your competition only if you are better than them.

I am sure you have watched baseball, soccer, football or hockey play-offs. Have you ever wondered how a team that finished first in the regular season can get defeated in the first round of the play-offs by a team not nearly as good? Upsets are fun to watch but have you ever wondered why they happen? The answer is simple. The ultimate goal is to win the last game of the season. It doesn't matter how many you win or lose throughout the year, as long as you are still there when the play-offs arrive.

The sales campaign is exactly the same. As long as you are still there after the short list is picked. Like these sports teams, you can unleash your plan with perfect timing and accept the victory.

Knowing your competition allows you to build and implement strategies or game-plans that can take them by surprise and defeat them. It doesn't matter how good they are, you can still win if your strategy is superior. Anybody can win, anytime, anywhere, and don't ever forget that. You let your guard down for only a second and your competition will steal the victory from you.

Learn how to gain control and keep it all the time. Always know where your competition is and what they are doing. Know their weak points and capitalize on them as often as you can. Take over their relationships and welcome their work with open arms.

Through this work will arise opportunities. Throughout your sales career, your competition will generate many sales victories for you. You just have to be aware of this so you can accept them.

Your competition will be some of the finest people that you will ever meet. Always treat them with respect and they will return the favor. Your competition can actually win more business for you then they will ever win for their own company.

Summary

Give your customers what they want by building strong strategies to guide you to victory. Leverage the competitive strategies put in place by your company. Learn everything you possibly can about your competition in order to defeat them more times then they defeat you. Someone has to win, it should be you!

If you **Know Your Competition** you can effectively position yourself to win more than your share. Most of your competition will never know you, nor take the time to get to know you. Your competition will be fixed on winning and not focused on anything else. So too should you.

Win Process:
Know Your Competition

☑ Knowledge	What you need to win
☑ Perception	Your view only
☑ Compete	To do battle
☑ Competition	A road block or a hurdle
☑ Experience	What you get from losing
☑ Sales Person	A business soldier
☑ Successful Sales Person	A business leader
☑ Responsibility	When you take control

Win Notes: My Competition

Use this page to assess your competitive knowledge. What are your strengths? Where do you need to improve?

11 Self-Improvement

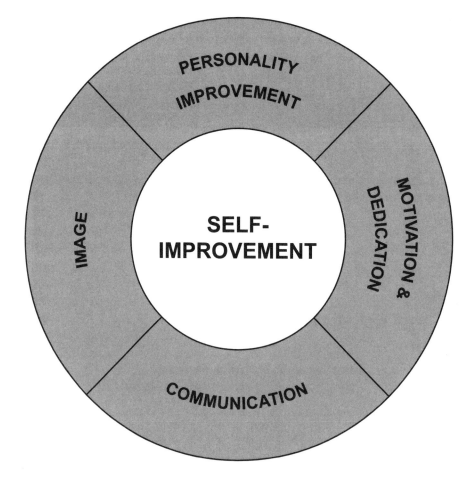

Self-Improvement

11

Self-improvement – what a concept! Believe it or not self-improvement doesn't get as much attention within the sales profession as it should. Sales Leaders believe in self-improvement but they are usually the only ones. They live by the adage, what got you to where you are today is no longer good enough to get you to where you need to be tomorrow. If you aren't improving yourself, how do you expect to keep up, much less become a Sales Leader?

The world is constantly changing. The products and services you sell change frequently. Your customers' needs are constantly changing. The company you work for is changing and evolving. So does it seem surprising that the sales profession must change as well?

And your change must be loaded with improvements. If you are not completing even simple tasks like attending sales courses, listening to audio sales recordings in your car or watching sales videos, you are being left behind. Everything I mentioned must be addressed just for you to stay close to average. There are many more complex improvements if you want to become a Sales Leader.

PERSONALITY IMPROVEMENT

Your personality may be the first item that needs to be addressed. There may not be anything wrong with your personality today but we must make sure that it doesn't get in your way. No matter what type of personality you have, there can always be room for improvement. It is up to you to continually develop your personality so you can get the most out of your business.

Before you can make improvements in your personality you should know how you and your personality are perceived by your customers and peers. The best and most direct way to uncover this valuable information is simply to ask your customers and your peers. Let's talk about your customer's view first.

Almost every customer will help you improve your personality as long as you are open to constructive feedback. Customers are very good at telling you how they would like you to act when in front of them. There is a large benefit here for you if you take the time to listen to these customers. We all know that if you have a great relationship with a customer, you will receive more business from them. It only seems logical that you take their advice to improve your relationship with them.

Win Tip

Don't be satisfied with what you know or have today because tomorrow it will have less value.

The next time you are with one of your customers, ask him or her to tell you one thing you can change in your personality that will help to improve your relationship with them. They will almost always give you an answer. Ask every customer you meet what you can do to change or improve your personality to better fit your relationship with them. You will be amazed at the feedback. This is all positive input that will benefit you in the future.

Maybe you have a great product with all the benefits of low price, fast delivery, longer warranties and whatever else customers think important. Now you have a great opportunity to involve your customers to the point where they teach you how to introduce, present and sell your product to them. I said earlier in this book that your relationship with your customers will dictate your success in sales. The better your relationship with your customers, the more successful you will be.

The same holds true for your co-workers. We all have weak points that need improvement and rather than not knowing what yours are, it is better to ask their views on your improvement. Not only does it make you a better person, it builds respect from both sides. You gain respect from them because you are asking them for help. They gain respect from you because you are implementing their ideas and comments.

Be a nice person. Be happy when you are around your customers. This is an area where many sales people could use some improvement. How many times have you dealt with a sales person and found they are very unhappy in their job? How did this impact their behavior? When a sales person is not happy they won't be nice to you. If a sales person is not nice to you they won't sell you anything. When I run into a sales person that isn't nice to me, I take my business elsewhere. Some of the best sales improvements will derive from just smiling and being nice. You've heard the expression, nice guys finish last. The exact opposite is true in the sales profession.

Have you ever run into someone who never agrees with anything you say or do? These people exist and you will run into them regularly. It takes months and sometimes years to build the perfect relationship with a customer. That can all be lost with one disagreement. If you are one of these people then you must make an improvement or you will get left behind. Learn to treat your customers with respect and always remember that he or she is, in fact, your customer.

Another way to improve your personality is to understand and empathize with your customer. It is far better to have issues with your own company than it is to have issues with your customers. Typically, issues with your own company get solved. Issues with your customers can linger forever. Learn how to quickly resolve any issue that arises with a customer.

MOTIVATION & DEDICATION

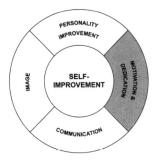

Improving your motivation and dedication is one of the best gifts you can give yourself, by opening doors to greater success than you ever had before.

Your prerequisite for this will be your strong will to succeed. You cannot be comfortable with status quo. If you are comfortable with your efforts and you are not a Sales Leader, someone needs to light a fire under you.

It is extremely tough to improve your self-motivation and dedication. I follow this rule when it comes to my success: never be satisfied until you are satisfied. These seven words make a powerful statement. If you live this rule, you are constantly setting yourself up for optimum performance. Can you imagine for a moment, optimum performance all the time?

Let's make sure we have a clear understanding of this rule before we go any further. Usually you become satisfied about something because someone has convinced you to be satisfied. In many cases where this happens, you are actually not satisfied, but rather, comfortable. You don't want to be comfortable in this situation. You must be motivated toward ultimate satisfaction. You must get to the point where you become satisfied – not just comfortable – with the results, whatever they are. Then, and only then, will the rule be effective.

Win Tip

When things get tough, go back to basics.

One of the most powerful factors behind motivation and dedication is focus. Know where you are going and why. Create a vision of what the end result will be and what steps you will take to get there. I once worked with a sales person who was totally focused every minute of every day. He would not involve himself in any sales project unless he completed an analysis of the particular project and decided he could focus his efforts and win the business. If he could not convince himself that victory would be the result, he would not proceed any further. He would find something else to focus his time on. Needless to say, this salesperson was extremely successful. He only chased what he knew he would win.

There are many sales people who have little or no focus. They lack motivation and dedication and become less than successful. In Chapter 6 we talked about working at a job that you like verses working at one that you don't like. If you don't like your current job, find a better one.

How can anyone be motivated and focused on success if they do not like their job? How can you actually get ahead when you hate getting out of bed in the morning to go to a job you have no interest in? Find a job that makes you feel good about yourself. We live in an environment today where you can attain whatever you want. Finding the right job in the right company is only the first step. Then you can work your way toward being fully motivated and focused for success.

ELRUDE

One day Jack Coleman learns about a customer looking to make a purchase. He contacts the customer and is quickly told there is no interest in buying anything from Jack's company.

Jack continues to ask questions trying to understand why he is not being considered as a potential supplier by this customer. His customer simply felt one of Jack's competitors offered a better product for a lower price.

Elrude 11-1

Jack was not satisfied that his competitor could offer a product similar to his for a lower price. Operating by the rule of not being satisfied until he is satisfied, Jack presses on with more questions.

Finally, Jack learns his competitor provided this customer with a brochure and a price for the product. After a brief discussion Jack encouraged the customer to call the competitor and confirm the price.

Much to his customers' surprise, the price was wrong. The

competitor mistakenly priced the product far below the actual price. When the customer called the competitor and asked for clarification, the price was quickly adjusted upward. This change caused the customer to reconsider his thinking. He invited Jack to a meeting and discussion of his product.

A couple of days later Jack presented his brochure and pricing to his customer. Everything was looking fine except there was another sales person who wanted to present a price. Jack was trying hard to convince his customer to give him the order and not entertain any other pricing.

Elrude Noclue called his customer six times before he finally got to talk with him. He immediately asked if he could give his customer a brochure and pricing but the answer was no. When Elrude asked why, he was told this customer was buying from another competitor.

Elrude has never heard of the concept about never being satisfied until he is satisfied so he simply thanked his customer for nothing and went off to lose another sale somewhere else.

Jack Coleman won again and this time he certainly was not satisfied until he was satisfied.

One Sunday afternoon I went into my office to pick up some documents. Over half my staff were there working while the office was closed. At first, I smiled and thought to myself I have a great bunch of highly motivated people working for me. I was right, but there is more than that. After talking with a couple of these dedicated individuals, I realized their job was a large part of their lives. They loved their jobs so much that they just couldn't stay away. Some of them had even brought their children with them.

I was very impressed my employees would come in to work on their day off. I was more impressed because they were doing it for themselves and not the company. They liked their jobs; therefore they have become extremely focused. They were producing results at an amazing rate and utilizing optimal performance through total motivation and dedication.

One more element of total motivation and dedication is setting goals and working toward them. Don't set goals if you have no intention of working toward them. You must want to set goals and work hard at achieving them or the process will be useless. Setting achievable yet challenging goals will help you focus on your work. It will also help you prioritize which task to complete first.

Set goals every day. Make yourself commit to attaining these goals all the time. The goals you set are more important than anything else that comes up. I have watched many sales people set goals but get sidetracked by things that come up. Average sales people will spend most of their time working on things that come up, compared to Sales Leaders who will work only on attaining the goals they set for themselves.

Win Tip

If you aren't improving yourself, how do you expect to keep up?

Be in control and always stay in control. I am sure you have heard the story about a person who has been driving an automobile for over twenty years without incident. One day he pulls out into traffic and gets into an accident. Upon interviewing that person, we hear him say that for the first time in his life, he lost focus and just pulled out into traffic without looking both ways. For twenty years, he has always been in control and never in an accident but for one split second he lost his control and smashed up his car. It doesn't matter what you do in life or where you are in this world, when you lose focus or control, you never know what will happen.

Win Tip

Sales Leaders are always on a self-improvement mission.

Don't let anything or anyone take away your focus for achieving your goals. You will deal with a constant barrage over your lifetime from people who are trying to upset your focus. I call them interferences. If you operate your entire work-day by addressing interferences as they come up, you will be less then average in sales. If you operate your entire workday by addressing and working toward your goals, you are on your way to becoming a Sales Leader.

COMMUNICATION

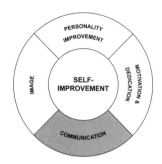

The area where I believe most self-improvement can be achieved is communications. I agree that many of the problems of the world derive from lack of proper communications. We have issues with our governments because of a breakdown in communications. We have marital and family problems because of a breakdown in communications. Countries have problems with other countries and movie stars have problems with the media all because of bad communications.

What's worse is bad communications between you and your customers. That will destroy your career. Continually improve your ability to communicate effectively by learning how and when to listen. Also learn when to speak and when to be silent.

Proper communication with other people allows you to stay motivated every day of your life. When you communicate clearly you are actually eliminating doubt and uncertainty that may arise later in the form of interference.

The third chapter of this book deals with communication, and we are talking about it again strictly because of its great importance for you and your success in sales. Many sales people have issues when it comes to listening. We are a strange breed of people who, for some reason, feel like we always have to be talking and telling people things. Of all the areas within the sales profession where self-improvement is needed, you will find communication is the one area where constant development must take place.

Sales Leaders listen all the time. The average sales person listens occasionally and usually for a very short time. As a sales person, you are not in control after you have given all the information away. You are in control only when you have the information. If you constantly talk and reveal items of interest about your product at the wrong time, you are in fact, giving your customer information he can use against you. For example, if you do not have a very good relationship with a customer and you tell him the price of the product you are trying to sell him, he just might go back to your competition and give them the news. They can now undercut your price and win the business.

The same holds true for product features. Whatever you tell your customer can come back to haunt you later in the sales campaign.

You must continually teach yourself the fine art of listening and only give out the information when your customer needs it for decision making purposes.

Say for example, you are watching a baseball game on television and your team has a runner on second base and a runner on third base and there are no outs. The next batter comes up and hits a small bunt down the third base line and successfully outruns the throw from the pitcher who ran in to scoop it up. You jump up out of your chair in amazement that a bunt would be called at that time in the game. The opposing team is bewildered as well. The game carries on and the next batter is a good home run hitter. He walks to the plate and points to the left field bleachers and takes his stance. The pitcher throws him four straight balls and the batter walks to first. The man on third scores and the bases are still loaded.

Can you see what is happening here? The team that is batting has full control of the game now because they took control away from the other team's pitcher. Not only did they take the control away from him, they put enough pressure on him that he has lost his focus and is now dealing with interference. Do you think the same scenario would have happened if the batter went out to the pitcher before the bunt and told him of his plans? The answer is no. The bunt wouldn't have been a surprise and the batter might not have made it to first base. The bases would not have been loaded. The home run hitter would not have gotten walked in four straight pitches. The runner on third might not have scored and so on and so on.

By keeping the information to themselves, the team that was batting was able to take control away from the other team and score some runs. My point here is this: When you give information away, it will cause you to lose control. The longer you can keep the information to yourself, the more control you can retain.

Relating this back to sales, don't give away any information unless it helps you move to the next step in the sales campaign. When you tell your customer about all your products' features without even knowing what they want or need, you are giving away your control. Learn to improve your ability to listen and understand first.

Also learn to read body language. There are plenty of books available on this subject. What does it mean when a customer is sitting back in his chair with his arms folded? What does it mean when a customer looks up and to the right? What does it mean when a customer looks at his watch? What does it mean when a customer won't look you straight in the eye? What does it mean when a customer has a purchase order out and a pen in his hand?

If you do not know how to read body language, you could be led down the trail of misery and defeat. This is not a place you want to go. Body language is more important than the spoken word. It holds just as much power as the spoken word but if you aren't watching for it you could miss very important information or reactions from your customer. This is an area that needs constant improvement. There are many great books available on how to read body language. I strongly encourage you to read one.

Win Tip

Becoming successful is rewarding but becoming continuously successful also offers stability.

Another area where constant care must be taken is accuracy of the information you are giving your customer. Make sure it is one hundred percent right or don't give them the information at all. It is easy to give an answer you think is right only to find later it was wrong and it cost you the sale. If you are the type of sales person who feels you need to know a lot about the inner workings of your product, then take the time to learn it rather than guessing each time you open your mouth.

Always have an understanding of what your customer requires from you. Don't assume anything. Listen carefully to their requests and answer them promptly. Anything less is not acceptable. Take the time to learn and re-learn how to listen. It is one of the most important skills you need to acquire to become a Sales Leader.

IMAGE

The final area of self-improvement is image. Previously, I talked about image and said it is one of the most important parts of the sales game. Your image can make the difference between winning and losing sales. At the beginning of this book I said your image can win or lose a sale for you during the first five minutes you are in front of your customer. Your customers' perception of you is extremely important. Improvement in this area is critical. Always make sure you are in style with your clothing and keep your personal hygiene up to par as well. Remember what helped to make you successful. It is this that will keep you successful as long as you are constantly aware of it and upgrading it.

Summary

Self-improvement is important in both our personal and business lives. We learn everyday about ourselves as well as other people. This new information causes us to rethink situations and can even cause us to act differently than in the past. Whether self-improvement comes in the way of something we see or something we think, it is always important to accept it. To be a better person, we need to work at becoming a better person. Don't become satisfied with what you know or have today because tomorrow it will not be enough. Never be satisfied until you are satisfied.

Practice **Self-Improvement** on a regular basis and you will stand out from the crowd. Average sales people become complacent and stop trying to improve themselves. Don't fall into this trap or you will fall behind. Sales Leaders constantly look for ways to improve themselves.

Win Process:
Self-Improvement

☑ Change	Expect more then one in your life
☑ Complex	What your selling strategy shouldn't be
☑ Improvement	Push it on yourself
☑ Achieve	Surpass average
☑ Keeping Up	Somewhere below average
☑ Feedback	Information needed for improvement
☑ Satisfaction	Somewhere above average
☑ Value	What you represent

Win Notes: My Self-Improvement

Use this page to assess your personality, motivation and dedication, communication skills and image. What are your strengths? Where do you need to improve?

12 Networking

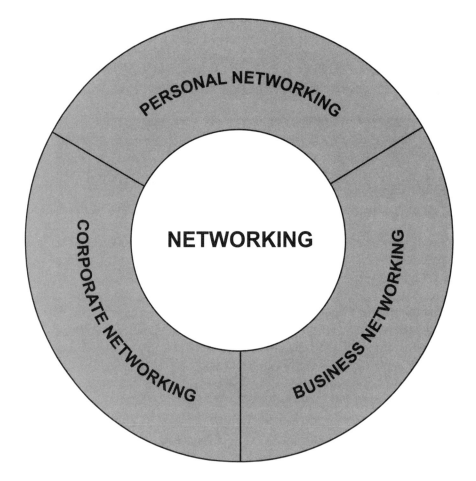

Networking   **12**

Networking is an important skill all sales people should develop and practice every day. It provides a starting point for many of the sales you win.

Networking helps you know who the customers are and what they're like, where the sales will come from, and what's happening in your profession. This is how you take in information and use it to be effective in sales.

You can always pick out a Sales Leader in a group of sales people. The Sales Leader is usually looking for more information. They are always asking questions. They seem to know more about you then you do about them. This is networking at its finest.

Win Tip
Networking is looking for and gaining more information than you currently have.

There are three types of networking. Personal networking involves what you do every day of your life. The people that surround you at work and at rest are all involved in your personal network.

Business networking still involves you but there is more of a direct relationship to industry groups in the area you are selling.

The final networking type is called corporate networking. This type of networking is a tag team event in which you partner with your corporate management.

Let's discuss how proper networking can help you become more successful in sales than you ever dreamed possible.

PERSONAL NETWORKING

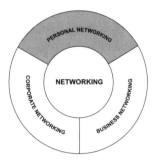

There is much information out there for you to gather and it begins right under your nose. The best place for you to start gaining knowledge about networking is to exhaust every avenue within your own office. Talk to your secretary or front desk coordinator. Get to know exactly what they do in their job functions. The reason for this is to uncover pieces of information they gather for other sales people in your office that could be effective in your own sales campaigns.

Find out which sales person receives the most telephone calls. See if they know how many of these calls come from customers and how many come from other business sources like breakfast club members or industry sales groups. Find out which sales person they complete the most typing for and what kind of typing it is. What types of letters do the other sales people send out? What other letters do they type and who else in the office sends out letters? There is a vast amount of information you can uncover simply by talking with your office secretary.

The reason you gather this information is to ensure you understand various ways to be successful. All people are successful in something. You are simply evaluating your networking data to find out what you can leverage for your own success. The more information you collect the better position you will be in.

Now it is time to start talking with other sales people in your own office. Most sales people love to talk about themselves so you should have no trouble getting information here. Make sure you speak with each sales person. They all have strengths and insights no matter who they are.

Have a list of questions ready for your conversations with your colleagues. Ask what they did to network when they started with the company. Find out how their networking helped them early in their career. Ask questions about their customers. How do they promote their product? How do they build a database of good contacts that might someday be their customers? All this is valuable networking. The fastest way to the top is to understand how the successful sales people have done it and do the same things. There is no sense reinventing the wheel if everything is right there in front of you.

The first five years of a sales person's life has the highest learning curve. Just think how far ahead of the game you could be if you took only one year to learn all that data and incorporate it into your sales campaigns. This is very possible if you take the time at the beginning of your career to network with everyone you possibly can.

Win Tip

Information is the fuel you need to win. Most of that information will come from networking.

Ask questions to everyone in your office. Don't be scared to ask your manager as well. It is interesting that at a time when you are allowed and expected to ask many questions, the exact opposite usually happens. New sales people usually accept whatever hand they have been dealt and learn by trial and error. I believe if you can accelerate this first learning curve by repeating the successes of the great sales people before you, your success will arrive quickly.

Many years ago when I was selling in the telecommunications industry, I networked with one of the installers. No other sales person did this to the extent I did because they assumed the technicians had no valuable information for them. They were certainly wrong with their assumptions.

One day during lunch time I went to a takeout restaurant in the same office complex and bought two fish and chip dinners and a couple of soft drinks. I took these dinners to the shop and offered one to this installer. We sat and ate our dinners together and while I was simply just trying to get to know him by asking a few questions, I uncovered more than I could have ever imagined.

During our conversation, he told me a great deal about himself and I realized he was a very intelligent man who had relationships with many people. He was one of those people you liked immediately. Over the next two months, he gave me many leads to chase. He built great relationships with many people who were in a position to buy telecommunication products. He just didn't feel comfortable giving these leads to any sales person until I came along.

I spent four years working as a sales person for that company and he was responsible for almost half my total sales. Networking played a large part in my success while I worked for that company.

ELRUDE

Elrude Noclue was called into his manager's office one day in the middle of the afternoon. He was asked what he knew about the Charlotte project and he replied nothing. He said he never heard of it before but if his manager wanted him to chase it, he would get right on it.

His manager was upset. The Charlotte project was one of the largest projects to come around in the last twenty years. It had just been awarded to Jack Coleman's company.

Elrude's manager did some investigating and found that Jack had been working on the project for almost three years. Obviously Jack had been well networked through all phases of his sales campaign. On this project, like all others, Jack followed a process. First, at a regular meeting with one of his industry contacts, he found out about the project. Then he utilized a variety of resources to understand this customers' business. He also networked with people in his own company who had experience in the past with similar customers. He also networked with selling strategists so he could put together a complete plan that enabled him to present an effective solution.

Elrude was amazed he had not heard of this project. How can Jack Coleman keep up, he thought. Certainly Jack was the type of sales person who hated to lose and Elrude wondered if he ever did lose at any time in his career.

Elrude's confidence was almost gone. It started to erode a long time ago and nothing has happened to change the direction. Elrude wondered if he was cut out to be a sales person. A few years ago when he entered this profession, he thought it would be a piece of cake and he would make quite a bit of money. He feels very different now. Elrude didn't realize how hard this job really was.

Another area where you should spend time networking is joining a sales breakfast club. You meet regularly with other sales people from non-competing industries. Everyone brings leads to each meeting to share with the others. For example, a commercial real estate agent may advise the group that XYZ Company is moving to a new building in six months. The telecommunications rep, the furniture rep, the business machine rep, the staffing rep and the commercial insurance rep would all be interested in this information.

While still in the telecommunications industry I joined a breakfast club with nine other members from various industries.

Win Tip
Increase your chances of winning.

I kept my ears open and usually brought in a couple of good leads for different people in the group. I would get the odd lead in return but they usually didn't seem to be very good. After meeting for almost six months, I told my boss I was going to quit this breakfast club and look for another one to join. He advised me to give the current group a chance and stay with it for a few more months.

Exactly four months later I received a lead from one of the club members. It didn't even come to me through the breakfast meeting. Instead, another member called me at my office one day and said he had a lead and the company was making a decision within two weeks. Our next club meeting wasn't scheduled for two and a half weeks.

I took the lead and started working it immediately. When I went into the next breakfast meeting I announced that I was victorious in selling this lead I had been given by a member of the group. This lead resulted in the largest sale I had ever won while in the telecommunications industry. It was valued at almost half a million dollars. My average sale in that industry was in the area of $25K, and my annual quota was $500K. You can see just how much this sale meant to retiring my quota and elevating my spirits.

Sales breakfast clubs can be rewarding but if you get tied up in the wrong club, it can be a waste of time. When you join one of these clubs make sure to get in with a solid group of people. By solid I mean dedicated, just like you, and make sure they all continue to show up for the meetings. There is nothing worse than belonging to a breakfast club with ten or more members but only three or four ever show up at any one time.

Remember to network in as well as out. We have just been talking about how to network out by utilizing other people and their knowledge to get the information you need. You also have information within your own mind that could be extremely valuable. Spend time by yourself every week and dig out all the inner thoughts you have about your business. During my entire sales career I have managed to remove myself from everyone for at least thirty minutes a day and go inside my own mind. Much of my selling success has started with my thirty minute creative networking meetings with myself.

People have asked me why I was so successful in a certain sales campaign and how I knew what move to make and when to make it. I outsold my competition because I took the time to sit down and network with myself. You see, as you go about your busy day your subconscious mind sees and hears information that doesn't immediately register with your conscience mind. You must sit down and interrogate your sub-conscience mind to get these ideas and thoughts out on the table. It is amazing what your mind digests in the course of a day. By networking within your own mind, you can uncover ideas and use them as strategies or tactics to win the sales you are chasing. Be a Sales Leader and practice personal networking.

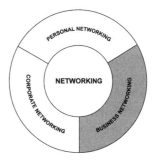

BUSINESS NETWORKING

Depending on the sales industry you work in, there are usually a number of industry groups you can join. I strongly suggest you join one or more of these groups and even work your way into the executive if you can. If you can become actively involved with an industry group, it will help establish you in that sales industry.

One of the benefits of joining an industry group is self-promotion. Your name gets around more and you are seen by many of your peers as a professional. It helps build your credibility when you put yourself into this position.

Another effective way to network is to read the news. Find all the available newsletters, papers, magazines and books and read them. Know everything about the industry you are selling into. Know as much as your customers – and for sure, know more than your competitors.

For example, if you sell residential real estate you should be reading:

- Which homes are listed for sale, which have been recently sold and for how much.
- Magazine and newspaper articles on housing trends in your area.
- Books on how to sell real estate.

Whatever material you can get your hands on, you should read. You can never fill your mind with too much information. The more you know, the better equipped you will be.

There will always be information out there that will help you become a better sales person. All you have to do is to search for it. Since my first day in sales, I have read everything I could get my hands on that was related to what I was selling. I remember times where I was reading about things I didn't sell because I couldn't find any new literature on what I was selling.

Networking is simply a way to source inward or outward to find information that will help you become more effective in selling. Make sure that you take the time to read for improvement.

Let's say you work in an industry where you have, on the average, three customer appointments a day. That works out to fifteen customer appointments a week. You now have unlocked fifteen more ways to network. Actually, networking with your customers is one of the best ways to uncover information. Where else can you learn where your price has to be, how long your deliveries should be, what color is needed, and so on? Your customer will always be one of your best networking sources.

Business networking is about finding ways to bring aboard new customers. It's an area where Sales Leaders thrive. Have you ever heard a top sales person say, after winning a large sale, that if it wasn't for his great relationship with his customer, he would have lost this to the competition? Through that great relationship he networked with his customer and found out all the information he needed to win the sale.

You can even take this to a further level and start networking with your competition. I have always done this and let me tell you why. First, most sales people don't like talking to their competition. It makes them feel uneasy. I love to walk right up and get in my competition's face. The first thing I always ask is how sales are going. The response I usually get from this question never ceases to amaze me. Try it.

You must be careful when you are talking with a competitor. Never give them more information than they give you. You will be surprised at what you can dig out of a competitor simply by asking. Be careful here though, experienced sales people can extract information out of you before you realize what you just told them. The secret to networking with your competition is remaining in control. There's that word again. If you are in control, they are not, so you can decide what you both will network about. You will feel comfortable and your competitor won't. Just maybe they will say something they didn't mean to and you win. All is fair in love and networking.

CORPORATE NETWORKING

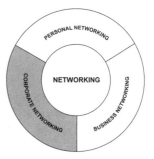

You shouldn't have to network alone. Your company must be in a position where they can network right along with you. Senior people in your company can use their networking expertise to cover people higher up in management within the companies you are networking with. An example of this would be while you are meeting and networking with your contacts, your company president or vice-president is meeting or networking with the customer's president or vice-president. This is corporate networking at its finest.

This approach is hard to defeat, if it is done correctly. The senior people in your company must rally behind you and network as well. It is one more way to beat your competition.

In recent times there is an acceptable approach to selling and networking that involves 'C' level contacts (Chief Executive Office, Chief Financial Officer, Chief Technology Officer, etc). This new networking tactic has generated great success for the sales people who are using it.

The business world has become more casual over recent years and this has allowed sales people to network more effectively with higher level customer management. It seems today that with companies downsizing, many customers don't have the staff to greet sales people and obtain all the information from them. In essence, there are not enough people left within the customer base to effectively network with all the sales people that are interested in networking. Business still has to move forward even though there are less people working with these companies. Someone has to network with the outside world and we find today that more and more senior management are networking with sales people.

Many doors are opened when you meet with senior management. They can and usually do make quick decisions. Make sure you are well prepared when you are in networking situations like this. Don't forget who you are meeting with. Credibility and trust are built or destroyed much faster when you are meeting with senior management.

Another area where your company can help you is by publishing newsletters and marketing bulletins. This is a great way to network with all your customers. You should also deliver these bulletins to industry groups and friends and others whom you feel may be of importance.

Sending out marketing literature is a great way to network outward. It doesn't matter if you send out one or two pieces of literature to a selected customer or if you send large quantities to many customers, you are networking, and in a way that is very important to you and your customers.

I network with hundreds of customers every month by sending out a newsletter I write. This newsletter offers information on my products and services as well as other informative and important data. I believe my newsletter is responsible for opening doors to millions of dollars of business. Networking is an area where you potentially create interest in whatever it is you are selling, while at the same time generating names of people who could potentially buy from you at some point in the future. My monthly newsletters generate many incoming phone calls inquiring about specific items I mentioned in my newsletters.

The last area of corporate networking is forming alliances or partnerships with your customers. When you utilize this type of selling, you are in effect, opening many new doors to potential sales.

Networking usually starts happening after the partnership or alliance is in place. These working relationships are usually set up to be win-win for both parties. You should network with each other to effectively bring out the true value of the relationship and to drive it to the ultimate success.

Summary

Networking is extremely important for any sales career. Networking is about listening and talking. When you network, you are opening yourself up to a world of choice and success. Just think how you would approach selling if you never used any of the networking tactics we just discussed. Networking has become one of the largest keys to our success as sales people. The sales person with the most information is in control for now. Hopefully the rest of their sales skills will maintain that control and push them on to victory.

Networking is a valuable tool to use in all your sales campaigns. Its value is measured in information rather than sales. However, in the end your sales will increase because of the information you have gathered. Networking is another way to be more successful in sales. You should make it part of your effort and use it constantly.

Networking means obtaining important information that will lead you to victory. There are many ways to find out about potential selling situations. You must know about these so you can add them into your backlog to chase.

Win Process:
Networking

☑ Management   Where answers come from

☑ Valuable   What you are to your company

☑ Association   Something you should belong to

☑ Effective   Works well and offers positive results

☑ Literature   Full of information

☑ Strength   Knowing more then your competition

☑ Insight   Leveraging your channels

☑ Breakfast Club   A place where information comes from

Win Notes: My Networking

Use this page to assess your networking effectiveness. What are your strengths? Where do you need to improve?

13 Setting Sales Goals

Setting Sales Goals 13

Setting sales goals will be one of the most important tasks you will undertake as you move toward Sales Leadership. Sales goals are not just set once and then forgotten. They are constantly modified and updated. Your sales goals will push you to the greatest success you could ever imagine. But setting goals is only the first step. Following them through to completion is what will bring the success you are looking for.

I have watched sales people wander through three or four years of undirected sales efforts only to fail in the end. I often thought about what would happen to these sales people if only they took the time to set and accomplish some goals.

I remember one sales person I met many years ago. He was an intelligent individual and in my mind, could sell in any industry. He was not lazy by any means and he usually worked hard at whatever he was selling. But he never set any goals in his career. He never knew where he was going next, nor did he keep a record of his many achievements. He just seemed to float along from sale to sale, from company to company and from industry to industry. Finally he moved to another part of the world and I lost contact with him for almost five years.

Win Tip

To be successful in sales, you must set goals.

When I met with him shortly after he returned to the city in which I live and work, I noticed that he had changed. During his time in another city, he worked for a variety of companies and each time, his career spiraled further downward. He interviewed well but his actual performance became dismal. He told me that he didn't know what to do or where to turn. One day, he read a selling newsletter that his manager had put on his desk and a comment caught his eye. The comment was a one line statement that read, 'Whether or not you set goals for the next year, you will still be a year older.' He said that was the turning point in his life. That one-liner took his breath away and made him realize he had been wasting time all these years.

His return to my city was short lived because his results started to soar and he was offered a management position in yet another city. I recently talked with him and he is still on a steady path forward. Learning how to set goals was the best thing that ever happened to him. As I look for great sales people to hire, he continually comes to mind.

There are sales people out there just like him but they continue to be average or even below average when they could be near the top in their career if only they would set some goals and follow them through.

Once you start setting goals in your business life you can carry that habit over to your personal life to improve your total lifestyle. There are four main types of goals you need to work on in the sales profession. These are the goals that enable you to attain your personal quota, progress to handling better accounts, achieve promotion and have a rewarding career.

ELRUDE

Elrude Noclue has just been called into his managers' office. It is early in the New Year and his sales manager is discussing sales goals for the coming year.

Elrude is asked what his sales goals are for the year and his reply was he didn't have any. At least he was honest. Elrude's manager questioned Elrude trying to find a reason why he didn't have any goals. Elrude couldn't give him a reason other then he just didn't have any. He was just going to see how things go.

Elrude's manager was appalled at his response. He quickly said that maybe he should not pay Elrude anymore and just see how things go.

Elrude's first rude awakening just took place. He finally realized that if he didn't contribute to the company, he would

Elrude 13-1

Let's set a goal to achieve this...

Yikes! I can't sell that much!

not get any contributions in return.

Elrude's manager came up with a plan. He knew Elrude needed lots of help and he wanted to see Elrude succeed. He set a goal for Elrude for the year. All Elrude had to do was retire a small quota. That would be his single goal for the entire year.

Elrude's first thought was this will be too easy but after a moment realized that he had never achieved his quota in the previous six years. He'd never come close and in some years he didn't sell anything at all. To actually make his quota this year will be hard. He agreed anyway and Elrude and his manager shook hands.

SALES GOALS FOR PERSONAL SALES QUOTAS

One of the most important functions in sales is to exceed your quota. This sets the standard for everything else you do in your company. Back in the first chapter we talked about creating an image. Your image as a Sales Leader will quickly disappear if you can't even meet your sales quota.

Your personal quota is the most important sales goal for you to attain each and every year you are in sales. That is how you are measured and evaluated. Of course, there are many goals that are important for you to surpass but the personal sales quota is the most important. If you attain your quota, chances are good you get to keep your job for another year. I know that sounds harsh but it is the case with many companies.

Win Tip

Be proactive for the future but focus on the present.

Each sales person will have a quota. Does this mean that each sales person is good at setting goals? The answer is no. Your quota is usually the only sales goal that is not set by you. It is handed to you by your employer. Once you know your quota, set other goals for how you are going to attain this new business. This is where you should start working toward optimum performance.

Optimum Performance

Optimum performance simply means going that extra mile. You will know when you are an optimum performer because you will not be satisfied with average performance. You will always be driving yourself and your team to finish first. You will have a desire to succeed that will be almost uncontrollable. You will understand the concept of winning. After all, isn't winning the result your company is looking for from you?

Win Tip

If you don't set goals today, next year you will still be a year older.

Optimum performance is used by anyone who is or desires to be a Sales Leader. Set and achieve your goals with optimum performance in mind and you will have nothing but success in your career. Many years ago when I first entered the sales profession, I decided I would use optimum performance in everything I did. I actually have trouble understanding people who seem to be just as happy to do their job rather than trying to succeed to the best of their abilities. People have so much potential but only a few ever tap into it.

Have you ever stopped to wonder why some sales people can sell so much more than others? Is it because they communicate better? Do they have better customer relationships? Are they more organized? The answer is yes, all that and more. Optimum performers focus on accomplishing the goals they set for themselves. That is the secret to their success.

Optimum performance is something you should embrace for yourself. During your career as a Sales Leader you must decide what average is for you and then work to improve your performance to a level high above that mark.

Win Tip

Set sales goals, write them down and tie a completion date around them.

Let's say, for example, you were a sales person selling packages worth twenty-five thousand dollars each. Let's also say that you sold an average of two of these packages a month. What would you think if someone told you that three years later you would sell a product valued at over forty million dollars in a country halfway around the world to a customer in a completely different industry where even the spoken language was different?

Well, I know a time many years ago when that actually happened. Of course, most of us don't read into the future but, knowing our own skills and the desire that goes along with them, I for one, would not have been surprised had someone told that to me. That is because I know I am capable of selling anything if given the chance. I have always believed in optimum performance and so should you.

Be in Control

You must always be in control if you plan on exceeding your goals. We have talked about this magical word on a few occasions already in this book and I am sure we will bring it up more times before you get to the end. You are in charge of your own life and everything within it. You must be in control of your sales volume to ensure you exceed your personal quota.

We have now brought three important terms to the table for discussion. We have talked about optimum performance, exceeding quotas and gaining control. No matter where you are in the sales world, living these three terms will drive you to success. You just have to keep doing them over and over again.

When you start in sales with a company, you may inherit a cold territory. It is up to you, using everything you have learned, to grow your territory and prove your value to management. Let me give you an example. A few years ago there was a sales person whom I perceived to have the ability for success but he didn't have enough accounts to really keep himself busy.

Win Tip

When you set goals, you are taking control of your career.

Another sales person who had been with the company for a longer time, offered to give up part of his territory, as he wasn't getting much business from it and thought it would fill up the first reps' spare time. I approved the transfer and very quickly an amazing event unfolded. When the first sales person was looking after this territory the total yearly sales were about one hundred thousand dollars. The first year that the new sales person was looking after the territory the yearly sales grew to over one million dollars!

I spent time trying finding out why the second sales person had more success than the first and this is what I found. The first sales person never set any goals. He never worried about exceeding his quota, as a matter of fact he was quite happy just to reach his quota. This sales person was not in control of his territory.

The sales person who took over the territory showed to me as well as the rest of his team that he was in control. Because he was in control he had no problem exceeding his quota or any other goal he set. He was definitely an optimum performer. He later added more territories into his sales area with similar results.

Later, he told me his overall goal was simply to get better and larger accounts to call on. He thought if he exceeded his personal quota with the territory and the accounts he was assigned, then he would earn the right to handle larger accounts. I agreed. He was such an optimal performer that he couldn't stop there. So he pushed himself on to the next step -- a promotion. No matter where he goes in any company, as long as he continues to demonstrate optimum performance, he will continue to be successful.

SALES GOALS FOR BETTER ACCOUNTS

Once you have attained your first set of goals it will be time to work on your second group so you can push yourself to the next step in your career. Don't just set one or two big goals for the year. Set a number of smaller goals. That way your personal satisfaction will be consistent, and you maintain a high level of personal motivation. One of the common traits I see in Sales Leaders is instant gratification. They like to accomplish goals and be recognized and rewarded for them regularly. This gives them tremendous motivation.

Once a goal is attained you should celebrate it and replace it with another. In sales, when the year is complete, you will always be given a new quota for the next year. Your new quota will probably be higher then last year's quota. This will set a new challenge or a new goal for you to attain.

After you have been selling for a few years and exceeding your goals the next logical step would be to take on some larger customers or higher revenue generating accounts. This seems to be a natural path for most sales people no matter what industry they are selling in. Some sales people will climb the company ladder faster then others. Setting and exceeding your goals that are based around your quota will become a determining factor on how fast you climb the ladder.

It is very important to your sales career to continue using optimum performance. It works like the gas pedal in a car – when you push the pedal down, the car moves forward. The farther you push the pedal, the faster the car moves. Optimum performance for a car is when the gas pedal is pushed to the floor.

It works the same way for you. The moment you stop using optimum performance you get the same result as when you take your foot off the gas pedal. Optimum performance slows down, and, like the car, will coast to a stop. You must keep your pedal pushed to the floor throughout your entire sales career.

The minute you take your foot off the pedal is the time when your career starts to slow down. And we all know that it takes much more effort to get a vehicle up to cruising speed from a dead start than it does to keep it cruising at its optimum speed.

When you move up the sales ladder you get bombarded with many new dilemmas. You must be in a position of control and deal with these dilemmas. The key word here is control. Whenever you start something new it is important for you to be in control. Remember we said earlier that without control you will have no impact on the final decision. In sales you need to be in a position where you have an impact on the final decision. If you are not in control, all your work could be wasted and one of your competitors will most likely win.

Win Tip

With every task there must be a goal.

You will receive new quotas as you work your way up the sales ladder. As you take on new and larger accounts your quotas will increase. You must exceed these quotas as well or you will jeopardize your image, which of course will have an impact on your control, which will have an impact on your success, and the circle continues. Always exceed your quotas – period.

While working your way up the sales ladder you will find many hurdles to jump over along the way. Typically, you will start off with small accounts and as you become successful selling in this area, you will pass those accounts to the new person and you will obtain larger accounts to work on. That cycle could happen two or three times before you get all the large accounts. This is where you can really make an impression.

The goals you set for yourself at this time should position you for a promotion. Always be trying to move up. It is amazing the doors you can open for yourself if you just try. You can walk down a long corridor with many side doors and if you never try to turn any of the knobs, you will still be the same person at the other end of the hall. If, on the other hand, you try all the doors, maybe your promotion will be behind one of them. You will never know until you try.

SALES GOALS
FOR PROMOTIONS

Now you have succeeded to the point where you have just been promoted. Maybe you are still directly in sales and maybe you are a manager. It doesn't matter where you are at this point as long as your promotion has taken you to a new level in your sales career. Now you must start the process all over again.

Win Tip

How do you know where you are going if you don't set goals?

Address actions with optimum performance again. Use whatever it was you used to get you here, to get you to the next step. Chances are that you will now have a new learning curve. Proceed up this learning curve very quickly and the only way to do that will be to set more goals and work toward them as fast as you can.

It is now more important than ever that you gain control because as you move up the ladder and take on more important tasks, the control factor will be worth more. Never give this control away to anyone. Maybe you will earn a series of promotions over your sales career and when you retire you should fully believe you gave it your best shot. You are responsible for you future so when it comes time for your retirement, you will be responsible for your past as well.

Win Tip

Learn how to build a game plan.

Setting and achieving proper goals today will ensure your future needs will be met. Setting and achieving goals today will move you into a successful position on your way to becoming a Sales Leader.

SALES GOALS FOR
A REWARDING CAREER

A rewarding career is the result of many years of hard work. When you look back and can honestly say you had a rewarding career in the sales profession you must have completed many things right.

All through this chapter you read about optimum performance and the benefits it brings for you. We discussed many reasons why you must use optimum performance all the time. I said earlier that average is not good enough. An average sales person would never be hired on my sales team. I have room only for Sales Leaders who use optimum performance.

Another reason you should use optimum performance is you could easily double or triple your income. Apply yourself and always try your best. You will find more success with this type of approach.

Let's review exceeding your personal sales quotas. This is important in the selling world. If you can't exceed your quotas, you will never be able to advance your career. If you can't exceed your sales quotas, a lot of doors will be slammed in your face. Don't get comfortable with just reaching your quotas. Get in there and work hard to exceed them.

The final term I want to review is the aspect of control. I have mentioned already in this book that if you have no control then you have no influence on the decision in the end. You could work an entire sales campaign only to lose it because your competitor had control. The same holds true for your sales career. You could lose a potential promotion because you never took control of your own situation.

Summary

Once you work your profession with the attitude that you will be fully in control then you can set all the goals you want. Once you set your goals and work toward them you can exercise optimum performance to ensure you reach them. Optimum performance will also help push your career so you can exceed all the quotas that are placed upon you.

When you are retired and sitting on the hotel sundeck in a resort town overlooking the ocean with a golf course in between, remember it will be the four terms in this chapter that will have enabled you to be on that deck. You will be able to sit back and think how great it was to be a Sales Leader.

Setting Sales Goals is the only way to exceed your quotas. You must set goals, otherwise how do you know what to do and where to go? Set solid, attainable goals that will represent a challenge for you and help you develop into a Sales Leader.

Win Process:
Setting Sales Goals

☑ Successful   When you continually win

☑ Exceed   Better then the rest

☑ Goals   Reasons to come to work

☑ Sales Goals   When you strive for excellence

☑ Tactics   Pieces of a plan

☑ Attain   Reach your goal

☑ Quota   Something you set sales goals to exceed

☑ Optimum Performance   Going that extra mile

Win Notes: My Sales Goals

Use this page to assess your sales goals. What are your strengths? Where do you need to improve?

Section 2: Practicing the Game

Summary

Practicing the game deals with forgotten pieces of the selling puzzle.

Many sales people lose focus about what they want to accomplish. Sales Leaders continually build and follow personal and business plans.

Develop and maintain rewarding customer relationships. People buy from people they know and like. Your success should not rely on your name being picked out of a hat.

Finding the right balance between our business life and our family life can be extremely difficult. That's why it's so important to be in control of our lives. Putting in all the time necessary to get proactive will usually mean less time is required to stay proactive.

Understand how competitive differentiation works for you and your competitors. Know how to use it, how to spot it, and how to sell against it.

The expression 'change is the only constant' is never more true than in sales. If you don't embrace and stay ahead of change, you will be left behind – period.

Networking is expanding your base of knowledge and contacts. Do whatever you can to meet people. Also enlist your senior management to network for you. Peer networking at their level can be very valuable to your sales success.

Sales Leaders practice the game before they play it.

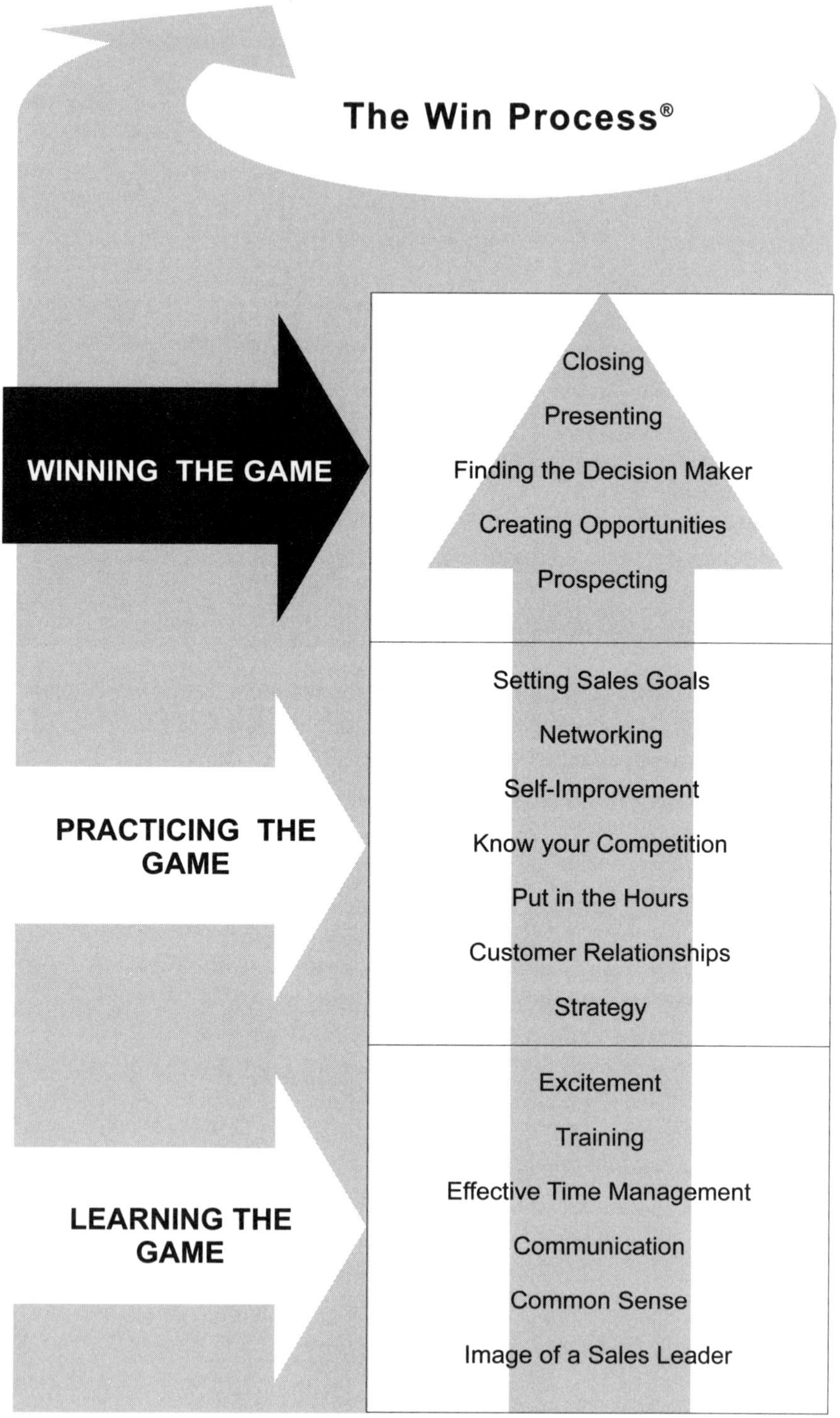

The Win Process®

WINNING THE GAME

Closing

Presenting

Finding the Decision Maker

Creating Opportunities

Prospecting

PRACTICING THE GAME

Setting Sales Goals

Networking

Self-Improvement

Know your Competition

Put in the Hours

Customer Relationships

Strategy

LEARNING THE GAME

Excitement

Training

Effective Time Management

Communication

Common Sense

Image of a Sales Leader

Section 3:
Winning the Game

Introduction

Now we are ready to get into the real study of the sales game – acting and thinking like a Sales Leader. Before you read any further, make sure you fully understand the previous two units. If you don't have a plan formulating in your head about your future success, stop now, go back to the first page and start again.

Mastering this section will be demonstrated by your ability to:

- Understand how continual **Prospecting** is key to your sales success
- Proactively look for ways of **Creating Opportunities** in your territory
- Know how important **Finding the Decision Maker** is to your win ratio
- Inspire commitment when **Presenting** your solution
- Be **Closing** every step of your sales campaign

14

Prospecting

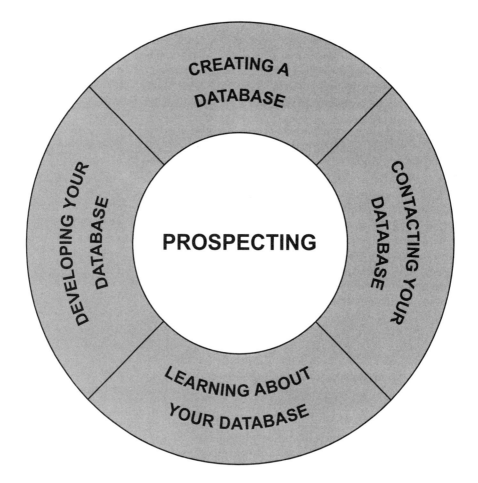

Prospecting

14

ELRUDE

Hi, it's
Jack Coleman
calling...

Elrude 14-1

Jack Coleman doesn't mind cold calling. Actually, he quite enjoys it because he sees the results of years of cold calling and how it has increased his overall sales numbers.

Each week he calls on people he has never met before at companies he has never sold anything to before. Over the previous six years Jack has gained many new customers for his company. He has been asked by other sales people what he does to bring in these new customers.

His story is always the same. When you bring in a new customer it usually means you contacted a large number of people you have never talked with before. If you contact enough new people you will eventually find someone who is looking for what you sell. From this point on the process is pure selling.

His cold calling process is simple. He finds names and phone numbers to contact and devotes a portion of his time each week to call the people and ask his questions. He receives a variety of responses – from interest to rudeness and everything in between. Rude people don't bother Jack. He doesn't have time to dwell on them. He would rather deal with the occasional rude customer than carry heavy objects in sub zero weather; because somebody does that job every day as well.

Elrude Noclue hates cold calling so much he almost never does it. He has not brought in any new customers over the previous six years, and his results show it. He sees no value in cold calling and continually refers to it as a no-value selling option. The few times each year his manager makes him call people Elrude gets so stressed out he takes a couple days off work to get rid of the headache.

His manager has been saying lately that he would like to get rid of a big headache too and he probably will soon.

Prospecting is contacting people who may have a need for your product. There is a myth about people coming to you if they want to buy what you sell. I agree this is a myth. Many sales people think selling is just waiting for phone calls, taking orders and making money. They are partially right. There are jobs out there where you can sit at a desk and take orders from customers. The job title for this is order taker and it usually pays about five or six dollars an hour. I am sure you can find many of those jobs if that is what you are looking for. But I believe you are looking for something more.

Win Tip

Prospecting is one of the hardest parts of the selling process. It's one of the most important as well.

There are four parts to prospecting: creating a database, contacting your database, learning about your database and developing your database. Following these steps will help you win new customers and new business. Let's get started with our first area.

CREATING A DATABASE

This is usually the area that creates the most anxiety with new and inexperienced sales people. What is a database and why is it important? A database is a list of names of people or companies who may one day become customers. A database is important because one of the truths about selling is that customers come and go. Nothing is certain. A valued customer of yours, who has given you a great deal of business in the past, could be acquired by a competitor of theirs, who buys only from a competitor of yours. Or your customer could change their business direction, or go out of business altogether. Don't rely on your existing customers for your future business. You need to accumulate the largest list possible in order to generate the success you will need in sales.

Before you just start adding names to a list, figure out who should be on this list. Basically you will need to find out who would have a need to buy whatever it is you are selling. Let me give you an example.

When I started selling in a new industry many years ago, I was given a geographic territory in a rural area within a few hours drive from the city in which I worked. No one in the office knew anyone in the territory so I had to go there and find out for myself. My goal was to learn the names of people and companies who might be in a position to buy my products.

I spent three full days in the country, driving up one road and down the next. When the three days were over, I had created a list of over seventy-five potential customers and one hundred plus individual names. I drew road maps of where all these facilities were located. Then I came back into the office and recorded my data. I logged all the individual names and addresses. Then I wrote a thank-you letter to each and sent them in the mail. What I had just created was a database of potential customers. During the eight years following that trip I sold almost seven million dollars worth of products to that original database.

It doesn't matter what type of territory you are responsible for, you must create your own database. Throughout this chapter we will learn how to develop your database and turn some of those names into happy customers.

This is where tactical selling starts. The more names you can get on your list, the greater your chances of success. Another way to get names on your list is to ask the veterans of your company for names of people they may have dealt with when they managed your territory. Usually they can come up with a few names of people who bought from your company in the past.

The idea here is to get as many names on your list as possible. This will be your database. I write a company newsletter and send it out regularly to over one hundred people who are on my database of names. No matter how long you have been in sales you should always use a database. Also, make sure you update your list regularly. A list that is not current has little value.

CONTACTING YOUR DATABASE

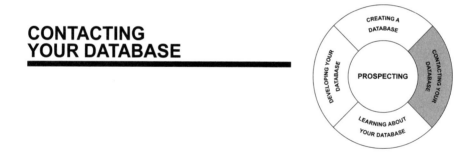

A database will not be of any use unless you put it to use. One of the first tasks is to send everyone on it a letter. This letter will be your official introduction. All you are trying to do at this point is get your name in front of everyone on your list. Your letter should be brief: tell them your name, your company name and what it is that you sell, and conclude with a statement that you will be contacting them at a future date. Be very careful about the date you pick.

I have witnessed many introduction letters sent out with a message the sales person would contact them within two weeks. For some reason the sales person never gets around to contacting the customer for a long time. By this time, the customer has forgotten he received a letter. Or worse, he remembers you did not honor your first commitment to him. Not exactly the way to begin a relationship.

I receive letters quite often at home from sales people who are just starting with insurance firms, real estate companies and other sales organizations. These introduction letters tell me the writer will contact me within a certain timeframe. Only one of those sales people ever honored that commitment. She now carries all our personal life insurance with her company. If you are going to go to all that work of building a strong database, take the time to follow it up properly.

If you give yourself two weeks to follow up with your introduction letter, make sure you follow it up within two weeks. Many sales people never follow up their introduction letters with any action. You must follow the strategy with a tactic or the strategy will be useless.

A few years ago, the company I was working with had outgrown their current office space. It became part of my agenda to search for larger premises. Three weeks previous, however, I received a letter from a commercial real estate agent introducing himself and highlighting several properties he represented. One of those properties appeared to fit my needs. He said in his letter he would definitely contact me within a week to discuss this new space. I never heard from him again. He lost a large sale before he had even started. We eventually moved to a different location and used another agent.

Once you have sent out your letters, follow up with everyone. Never send all your letters out at the same time and tell everyone on the list that you will contact them in two weeks. You would create a situation almost impossible to maintain. Send out a few letters each week, enough that you can realistically follow up. Do the same again next week and the week after that until your complete database has been covered.

Make sure you prioritize whom you will call first. This may be tough to do but, based on your knowledge of what is happening in your industry, consider which companies will have an immediate need for your products.

Once you have completed all this, it will now be time for the actual visit. Remember all the pieces we talked about in the first two units of this book. Your first five minutes in front of the customer will either set you up for a lasting relationship or it will be your last five minutes in front of that customer.

Make sure you ask questions and let the customer do the talking. Even if they are not in the market to buy something from you today, uncover as much information as you can in case there are future projects or decisions that may involve products similar to yours.

Go out and visit the people. You will not become a sales success by sitting in the office all day. Usually, companies will give a new sales person anywhere from three months to as long as a year to reach the sales level required by management. The higher value product sellers will usually have more time to ramp up compared to commodity sales people who should be up to speed rather quickly. In any case, you don't have much time to start performing in the eyes of your management.

Win Tip

Prospecting is the foundation of your selling effort.

Work your database as hard as possible. The aim of prospecting is finding customers who might buy your product. Dig up as much information as you can. A general rule of thumb is five percent of them will have an immediate need, twenty percent will have a need in the near future and another twenty-five percent will have a need over the long term. The remaining fifty percent may not have a need at all. That means there is business available; you just have to go and find it.

It also means you should constantly add names to your database or your potential for sales will run dry sometime in the future. Prospecting is just as important twenty years into your sales career as it is on your first day.

LEARNING ABOUT YOUR DATABASE

You have much to learn about your database, and the sooner you learn it, the better. You need to know who is in your database, what business they are in, do they have a need for your product, and which of your products can satisfy their needs.

First, you must learn about the people who make up your database. What are these people actually like? Are they open to you calling on them? Do they perceive you could possibly bring them any value or are you just wasting their time? Then you should learn about their business. What exactly do they do and how do they do it? Can your product replace an existing product or can your product revolutionize the way this customer does business?

Before you can sell anything to a customer, you must identify a need. In order to identify a need you should understand their business. Your potential sale derives from your customer's need to improve their business processes.

The next part you should learn about your database is which of your products or services apply to each customer. You should know enough about what you sell that when you are prospecting and digging for information, you identify where your solution can help the customer.

One more very important piece of information you must uncover from your prospecting is your chance of an actual sale to this customer. Obviously, if there is no chance of you selling something to this customer, there is no need for you to call on them again. You must go where the sales are.

DEVELOPING
YOUR DATABASE

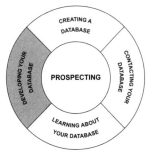

About half the names in your database will be in a position one day to buy a product you sell. Only a handful of those customers will buy anything in the short term. The majority of these customers will need to be sold. The next few chapters will deal with the issues and solutions to get you to the point where you and your customer both agree that your product is the best fit for them. The remainder of this chapter will show how to develop your database to the point where you can start a dedicated sales campaign by creating opportunities.

Critical to developing your database is maintaining contact with your customers. You have already established they are part of your database. You sent them a letter introducing yourself and in that letter you told them you would either call or visit them in the next few weeks. Then you met with them and asked questions as you tried to uncover a need.

Now you must go back and see them again. You must continue prospecting to determine if there is potential for a future sale. I will always remember a vice president with a company I worked for many years ago stating that when a customer says no, what they really mean is they don't know.

Win Tip

If no one knew how to prospect we would never have found gold.

Make sure your customers know about your company, about the products you sell, and about you. Provide them with brochures, your website and any other pertinent information. The key here is to maintain top-of-mind awareness with your customers. You want them to think of you first.

Prospecting is one of the most important parts of any sales campaign. Customers don't just come knocking on your door looking to buy something. Many great widgets were never given the proper chance to generate any success because the accompanying sales and marketing plan was flawed. The core of sales and marketing is getting out there in the field, creating awareness and closing deals.

There are sales people who are very good at prospecting and there are others who are better at closing sales. The idea behind this book is to improve all the areas we perceive we are not as strong as we should be. I once knew a sales person who was an excellent prospector. He met more people in a month than I could ever dream of meeting in a year. He had an innate ability to find contacts and put them in his database for future sales.

There are many sales people who are in the top ranking when it comes to building relationships, presenting themselves and their product, creating opportunities and closing. It takes more that a great sales person to be top ranked when it comes to prospecting. Digging up names and making cold calls to people you have never spoken with before is extremely hard to do.

Summary

Cold calls are one of the most important parts of prospecting and most sales people don't like making cold calls or prospecting. Sales people typically want to sell and not find people to sell to. We all know that without customers, we can't make any sales. And if we don't know how to prospect effectively, we won't have any customers. And if we have no customers, we have no business.

Even Sales Leaders don't like prospecting. But they do it, because they must.

Prospecting is the hardest part of the selling process. It is also the foundation of your selling campaign. Contacting people to see if they are interested in buying what you are selling is called cold calling. This represents the largest part of prospecting. If you want to be a Sales Leader, you must be good at this.

Win Process: Prospecting

☑ Cold Calls

☑ Directories

☑ Newspapers

☑ Trade Shows

☑ Internet

☑ Referrals

☑ Existing Accounts

☑ Magazines

Hateful but important

Late night prospecting

Coffee time prospecting

Having a good time prospecting

Very late night prospecting

Credibility prospecting

Base business prospecting

Once a month prospecting

Win Notes: My Prospects

Use this page to assess your prospecting skills. What are your strengths? Where do you need to improve?

15   Creating Opportunities

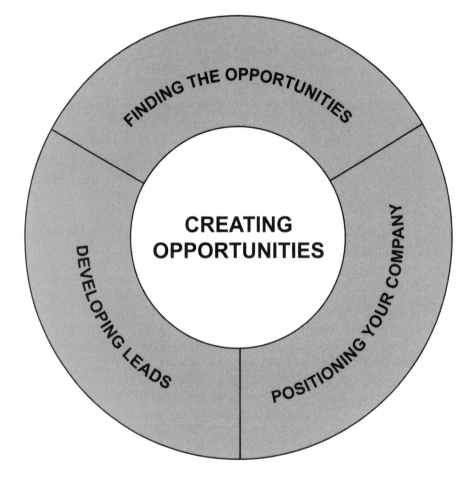

FINDING THE OPPORTUNITIES

POSITIONING YOUR COMPANY

DEVELOPING LEADS

CREATING OPPORTUNITIES

Creating Opportunities   15

Up to this point we have been talking about finding sales opportunities identified by the customer. But selling is more than just reacting to the queries of the customer. It's more than making sure you are on the bidders list. It's more than being at the right place at the right time.

FINDING THE OPPORTUNITIES

Selling also involves proactively looking for opportunities to help your customer do business better. It's providing solutions to problems the customers did not know existed. In order to do this, you need to understand your customers' business, industry, competitors, environment, and all the other factors that impact their ability to make money.

Some of you may be asking why you would want to go to all that trouble and effort just to make a sale. After all, if you have a good relationship and a good history with that customer, you will always be on the bidders list, right? Perhaps, but when you create an opportunity and provide the solution that can make a positive impact on the customers' business, you are creating value. And customers place a great deal of value on value.

Look at it this way – if you have taken the time to understand the customers' business, industry, competitors, environment, etc. and have proposed a solution that can positively impact their ability to make money, they are not about to discourage your creativity and value by taking your idea to bid. Most customers want partnerships with their vendors. Price and value are not synonymous. Price is the great equalizer. Value is the great differentiator.

I had the extreme pleasure to work with a sales person who created many opportunities through his career. I watched him many times sit with his customer and suggest a method of improving a process, and present a return on investment that inspired his customer to look further into the opportunity. If the customer agreed with the suggestion, he would approve the budget and place the order with my colleague. The opportunity never went to other sales people for competitive bids.

Win Tip

Creating opportunities is providing solutions to problems the customer did not know existed.

Situations like this occurred frequently for this sales person, and they generated more sales and revenue that helped to drive his success to a higher level. Also, because these situations did not involve the competition, more profit could be built into the sale without jeopardizing the outcome.

Creative Thinking

Finding opportunities is fueled by a creative mind. You don't necessarily need to know everything about your product or service but you do need to know how it can enhance your customer's business.

This approach also applies to retail selling, where it is not a customer process you are trying to improve, but your customer that you are trying to enhance. I will give you an example of this. I love buying dress clothes and I certainly have more then my share. I usually shop around for deals but I am somewhat loyal to a couple of men's clothing stores.

The more successful of the two sales people I deal with at these men's stores has taken it upon himself to fully understand what I like to wear. Instead of waiting for me to visit his store, he will call me from time to time and tell me about a new piece of clothing I would look good wearing. This prompts me to visit him and I will usually buy something even though it might not be the item he called me about. Over the past few years he has introduced me to new styles and new colors that I believe look good on me.

I usually wear colored dress shirts and up until recently I did not own a white dress shirt. He called me one day and suggested I come in and try on one of his new shirts. He created a new look I liked and I now own several white dress shirts, all purchased from him.

He has the ability to create an opportunity for a potential sale every time he calls me. He does the same for his entire customer base. This is selling at its finest. Anyone can sit behind a desk and take an order. Anyone can win a selling competition. But when you create your own opportunities, you can win profitable work for your company and at the same time construct a solid relationship built on value.

Referrals

Another way to find potential opportunities is by word of mouth. Sales Leaders are very hard to find, and when a customer finds one, word usually travels quickly. We talked about building relationships a few chapters ago. Well, it is relationships like this that help us find the opportunities that eventually turn into successful wins.

When you build strong relationships with your customers, you are opening up a flow of information that will help you become more successful. Sales Leaders use their relationships to help them stay on top of all upcoming opportunities as well as look for ways to create new opportunities wherever they can.

Once you have been successful in winning some of these opportunities and you have happy customers, it becomes time to get referrals. Obtaining referrals has been part of successful sales campaigns for years. Referrals can significantly increase your chances of winning your next sale.

Many customers do not have the time to shop around for the product or service hey need. They often ask a friend or business associate about their experience. If it was positive, the customer will likely buy from the same sales person. Remember – we learned earlier that people buy from people they know and like. You can see why getting referrals is important to your success.

Many sales people go about their daily business without utilizing all the sales tools they have at their disposal. They don't understand that part of their job is to create opportunities for future work.

I remember a sales person many years ago who was responsible for a large number of existing customers as well as a territory filled with potential customers. His job was to support the existing customers and gain new business in his territory. But he couldn't see the value of referrals or supporting his existing customer base. He felt that was a waste of time and he should be out on the street knocking on doors.

Win Tip

Business by referrals puts you on the fast track to becoming a Sales Leader.

Over the years he spent countless days knocking on doors. While he was out on the street trying to get in as many sales calls as he could, his competitors were building relationships with their customers and getting all the referrals. His competitors had created many opportunities in which he never participated. He never really knew what potential business existed in his territory unless, by some stroke of luck, he managed to knock on a door just as they were ready to buy something. Using this approach, he became involved only in competitive situations.

Referrals have become one of the greatest sources of sales revenue for Sales Leaders. I have a hard time believing most sales people do not leverage referrals, but the fact is – they don't. Referrals were responsible for at least half of all my selling victories.

In the game of selling you have two choices. Run around without any idea of what you are trying to accomplish, or use the tools you have in your sales toolboxes. Unfortunately, one tool that is constantly left in the toolbox is the instructions on how to create opportunities.

The Written Word

One of my favorite ways to create opportunities involves leveraging the written word. With the vast amount of information available today, this should be one of your prime prospecting methods. The two sources for this information are internal – what the company publishes about itself, and external – what others say about the company.

As part of your quest to understand a company, and how you can add value to it, read what they say about themselves by visiting their website, examining their brochures and paying attention to their advertising. Most companies will promote their differentiation – what makes them unique, and better than their competitors. Leverage this information. If your company sells a product or service that can help a company maintain or increase its competitive advantage, you have value. If your product can directly (i.e., increase their speed to market) or indirectly (i.e., decrease their costs so they can spend more on research and development) help your customer, you have value.

Also pay attention to what others are saying about businesses. If an organization is being trashed in the media because their customer service lines are always busy, and your company is in the contract call center business and can help by off-loading some of the incoming calls, you have value. Read the newspapers, magazines, trade journals, stock market reports and anything else that can give you an insight as to which companies may have a need for what you sell.

Win Tip
Creating opportunities gives you leverage.

Here's an example of how this approach can work in the life insurance industry. Selling life insurance demands a strong commitment to prospecting. This becomes a major focus of your daily activities. One day you read a newspaper article that states a company in your city is expanding one of their departments and will be adding staff. Your selling campaign becomes finding out who these new staff members are because once they start their new job, they will be strong candidates for your service. Then you must meet with them and convince them to buy your product. Many sales people don't do this or ever think about creating an opportunity like this.

The written word is equally applicable in business-to-business selling. Let's look at another example, this time in the manufacturing industry. A trade publication you are reading contains an article about a new manufacturing facility to be built. This written word sets the stage for a flurry of activity involving sales campaigns from many different suppliers and service providers. You consider not only the immediate and obvious opportunity, but also the future opportunities you could create. But first, you must win the initial contract.

You cannot effectively create opportunities when you are in a competitive situation. You can create a need but your competition may be able to satisfy the need as well as you, therefore it is a need and not an opportunity.

Regardless whether you win the project or not, one thing is for certain. If you don't chase it, you will not win it. If you don't know about it, you won't chase it. If you don't read about it, you might not know about it. The written word should not be taken lightly.

Win Tip

Sales leaders thrive on creating opportunities.

Take the time to read the written word and use the information to your advantage. Other opportunities can evolve from what you read. When you work in sales you must be constantly alert. Some sales people think selling is easy and they don't need to work hard to be successful. Sales Leaders know otherwise.

Remember, many sales people are simply order takers while others are quite comfortable to be involved in competitive situations. Only Sales Leaders thrive on creating opportunities for their customers.

POSITIONING YOUR COMPANY

Your company expects you to take a leading role in growing their business – that's why you have a quota. Always position you and your company for greater success. When you get down to the nuts and bolts, ask yourself what you can do to better position your company. Ask yourself how you can create opportunities to generate more business for your company and at the same time provide solutions for your customers.

Growth Opportunities

Each sales person must understand the value they can bring to customers and their own organization. We all start out as sales people the same way. It is what we accomplish once we start selling that determines if we become Sales Leaders. If you can favorably position your company with your customers, your goals will be attained much easier. Focus on what you can do to improve your company's position with your customers. This role is easily defined – add value.

When you add value to your customers, you will increase your sales. When you increase your sales, you add value to yourself within your company and the marketplace. Your competitors are always looking for Sales Leaders. There comes a point where they will get tired of losing to you. And the best way to neutralize a competitive sales person is to hire him. Your company executives know this as well. They want to hold on to their Sales Leaders.

ELRUDE

Elrude Noclue is meeting with a new customer for the first time. He got up late this morning and will not be on time for his meeting.

When he sits down in his customer's office, he can tell that his customer is not happy. Elrude immediately apologizes for being late and makes excuses for his tardiness.

Elrude talks negatively about some of the products he sells. He tells his customer not all of them are bad but some are. He also tells his customer he will guide him toward the good stuff. He believes this approach will win his customers' confidence.

After ten minutes with his customer the meeting is over and Elrude leaves. His customer is angry because he just wasted his time with Elrude. He couldn't believe Elrude's attitude. Elrude never even tried to promote his product. He felt quite content to bash his own company, products and services. The customer believes that Elrude wouldn't know an opportunity if it were standing beside him.
When Jack Coleman met with the same customer his approach was to listen, understand and then talk. Through this process

How did this guy ever find a job?

Well, I've got this sale wrapped up!

Elrude 15-1

an opportunity was created in Jack's mind and he simply asked more questions for verification. When he realized he was right, he moved to the next step.

Jack promoted his company and products in a positive manner and created interest with his customer. He positioned his company and leveraged the research he had conducted on this customer. He discovered what was important to this customer and qualified this information during his meeting.

When it came time for the customer to select his vendor, he picked Jack and never once did he think about Elrude. Across town, Elrude wasn't thinking about the customer either. As a matter of fact he had forgotten all about him.

Companies can manufacture excellent products but if they don't have successful sales people on their team to create opportunities to sell these products, neither will be around long. All companies need Sales Leaders to help them grow the company.

Whatever product or service you sell needs to be promoted. People you meet must know you sell something and understand the value it brings to them. Let's say you sell real estate and one Saturday you are in a coffee shop on the other side of town. A conversation unfolds between you and a person at the next table. You talk about the weather, sports, and maybe the coffee as well. After the conversation you pay your bill and wave goodbye to the other person.

After you leave, he asks the waiter if he could borrow a telephone book because he needs to look up the phone numbers of a couple of real estate companies. He has decided to sell his house and buy a new one. Only by coincidence and luck would he ever call you. Do you want your sales success to be based on coincidence and luck? You will not win many sales if you take that type of approach.

Tell people what you do. Use your creative thinking to create opportunities whenever you can. Why would you ever expect people to buy from you when they don't know you sell the exact item they need to buy today?

Let's check back in with our real estate sales person to see what would happen if he did mention his occupation to the gentleman at the next table. He would have created an opportunity for new future business. The gentleman's comeback may have been that he wants to deal with real estate people in his neighborhood and not from the other side of town. The sales person could answer by saying he has a house listed for sale not far from here and it has a long list of features. They are only asking this much for the house and that is a great price. The sales person hands him his business card and offers to show him the house. The real estate agent has just created an opportunity. It's really that simple.

Simple things like this get missed by many sales people on more then one occasion. Think how successful you will be by doing these little things right. Think how successful you will become by learning how to create opportunities.

Positive Perception

Positioning your company may be one of the most important parts of your strategy. Successful sales people know in order to position your company properly involves creating positive perception. Customers and clients want to hear positive feedback about your business, and about you. Your persuasive power – positive or negative – will greatly affect your ability to do business with these customers.

Positive persuasive power is the right course and the only course for Sales Leaders. Promote only the successes of your company. Why meet with a customer and discuss negative company issues? It doesn't make any sense, especially to your customer. Promote your successes from all the opportunities you have created over the years and you will be amazed at the results.

The final step for positioning your company is your enthusiasm. Get out and see your customers. Spending the day in the office doesn't cut it and therefore should not be part of the plan. Positioning your company is important. Remember that owning the ability to create opportunities within your customer base will enhance your level of success that could turn you into a Sales Leader.

DEVELOPING LEADS

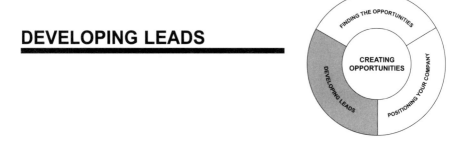

Value is in the eyes of the customer. If they don't think you are adding value to them, they will have little time for you. Understand their business. Learn their processes. Recognize their challenges. Only when you do this will you be able to create opportunities for yourself. How do you retain a customer? Continue to provide value. What is value to a customer? Ask them.

If you believe the adage that two heads are better than one, can you reasonably expect your customer will think of everything, and just call you when they want to place an order? Sales Leaders look for opportunities to create value in the customers' business, before the customer realizes there is a problem or a better way of doing things. Also, this is where you get to show off what you and your company can really do. Many times I've heard sales people say – 'I wish we could sell more of this, we're really good at it.'

Look for opportunities to match the core competency of your company to helping your customers. Those opportunities are out there, but they may not be right in front of your nose. Do some digging.

Company Direction

direction and core business, you are differentiating yourself from your competitors and positioning your company in the best possible light. Your company expects you to sell its products and services at a profit. Focus on your company's core products or services. This is where you will have the most leverage; this is where you can highlight your competitive advantage. And your best solutions will usually come from your core products.

Win Tip

Finding opportunities is fueled by a creative mind.

Many companies also resell products and services that have little margin. These are the products that generally cause the most grief. If you are reselling it, you don't control your costs. If you don't control your costs, you don't control your profit. If you don't control your profit – who does?

Usually, sales people who stick to selling their company's core products are more successful, but only if they have the ability to create further opportunities. The benefits to these sales people might be more income, promotions, self gratification, confidence, non-stressed environment and, most importantly being in a position to capitalize on all the opportunities you create in your business and personal life for you and your family.

Summary

There is a difference between prospecting for leads and creating opportunities. As we discovered in the previous chapter, prospecting for leads is finding someone who might be a candidate to purchase whatever it is we are selling. Creating opportunities is the task of moving these people into a position where they will purchase our solutions.

Offer more value to your customer. Create an opportunity for your customer where they require you and your product or service to fulfill their need.

The best way to generate success in selling is to sell your customer exactly what he or she needs or wants. How do you find that out? Ask them.

Creating Opportunities is part of the selling process that many sales people don't give much thought about. You should be able to create at least one selling opportunity every day you are working. Make this one of your goals and watch the impact it will have on your overall performance.

Win Process:
Creating Opportunities

☑ Impact	An advantage for you
☑ Watching	Gaining knowledge and information
☑ Positioning	Creating an advantage
☑ Leads	The seed of your harvest
☑ Solutions	The answer to winning
☑ Creative Thinking	A way to win more often
☑ Fast Track	Where creating opportunities will put you
☑ Leverage	The power you need to win

Win Notes: My Opportunities

Use this page to assess your skill at creating opportunities. What are your strengths? Where do you need to improve?

16 Finding the Decision Maker

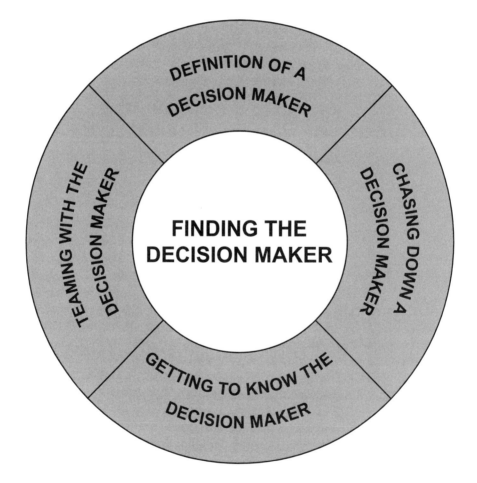

Finding the Decision Maker 16

Many sales campaigns end in defeat because the sales person never found the decision maker. Finding the decision maker will lead you to victory more often then anything else you will read about in this book. Has it been your experience that decision makers are often chameleons and can disappear for the entire sales campaign, only to reappear at the end, just in time to award the deal to your competitor?

Earlier in this book we mentioned that more people are empowered to say no than to say yes. And we all know how difficult it can be to change a no to a yes. In this chapter we will focus on defining, chasing, knowing and teaming with decision makers. But first, let's identify the three common scenarios about dealing with decision makers:

- Assuming you are dealing with the decision maker
- Being told by your contact that they are the decision maker
- Dealing with the actual decision maker.

The first two scenarios are time wasters. If you do not qualify and connect with the decision maker, your chances of winning the sale are slim to none. Not very good odds when your livelihood depends on your success.

DEFINITION OF
A DECISION MAKER

Who is the decision maker? How do you pick one out in a crowd? Well, the answer is simple. The decision maker is the lowest person on the customer's corporate ladder who can say no and make it stick.

When starting any sales campaign, you need to find out who will make the final decision. The type of sales campaign you develop is determined by what you are selling and who you are selling to. Should you be selling life insurance, finding the decision maker is usually very easy.

On the other hand, if you are selling a multi-million dollar integrated solution for an international customer, and you are dealing with numerous people in several countries, then you task of identifying the decision maker can be much more difficult.

Win Tip

Decision makers are often like chameleons and can disappear for the entire sales campaign

In these types of situations, egos can be your biggest obstacle. Many people have a high need to identify with power, or at least give the appearance they have power. They know once the decision maker is identified, the focus of the vendors will be directed elsewhere, and they will lose power and status. When you ask them who the decision maker is, they will usually say they are. What they are really saying is they have the power to stop you, but not the power to award the contract. This is why you will often hear they were overruled by someone higher up. Being upfront with you can make information gatherers feel they are losing face, so you need to allow them to save face and retain some control.

The best way to identify the decision maker and keep the information gatherers on your side is to ask about the decision making process. This takes the pressure off the information gatherers and in fact gives them an out if things start going bad. By asking about the decision making process you are acknowledging the roles of all the players. It's only natural then that you meet all the players. And if the information gatherers can facilitate that process, they maintain their status as an integral part of the process.

When I first began selling, I worked on a project for almost six months. I worked hard and what I also thought was smart but when decision day arrived, I was the most surprised sales person in the game. I hadn't even met the decision maker. I thought I did but it was the wrong person. I vowed then to never let that happen again.

Since my startling discovery I have watched my competition fall into this trap many times. It makes my work on the sale easier because I can almost guarantee my competition will do this over and over again.

There are two major reasons for finding the decision maker on a sales campaign. The first reason is you need the decision maker on your side if you plan to win. It would be difficult to get the decision maker on your side if the two of you never met. The other reason is for reporting purposes to your management. When your boss asks you questions about your sales campaign and who you are meeting with, he is not just checking up on you. He needs to know you are calling on the real decision maker. He knows if you are not in contact with the decision maker then your chances of winning the sale are almost zero.

Depending on the size of the sale and the size of the company, the decision maker can actually be a variety of different people. One thing for certain is every possible sale has the involvement of a decision maker. A small sale will usually have a decision maker lower down on the company ladder. A large sale will usually have a decision maker as high up as president of the company. A personal sale is less complicated from this point of view because usually you will deal only with one or two people.

Win Tip

Many people want to be decision makers, but don´t assume they all are.

In most cases the decision maker is only one person. That is the person you must get to know. That is the person who will ultimately decide to buy from you. The only exception to the rule is in some cases the decision maker can actually be a committee. It will, therefore, become important for you to get to know all the members of the committee. Although they may appear to have equal power for making a decision, one or more members could have more control and sway the vote. Know who these people are.

Decision makers are all different. Covering a decision maker can be extremely difficult. You should be prepared for almost anything. Some decision makers will be readily available and easy to get to know while others will be almost invisible and uncooperative. It will be up to you to chase down the decision maker. Don't miss this step in the sales campaign. It is one of the most important and is critical for your success.

CHASING DOWN A DECISION MAKER

Finding the decision maker on most business-to-business sales campaigns can be difficult, time-consuming and extremely frustrating. But the task must be completed because without contact, that decision maker will probably not be on your side.

Win Tip

Understand your customers' decision making criteria.

The real reason why some sales people can't put their finger on the success button is because they are unable to track down the decision maker. Many sales people will give up after a couple of attempts to make contact and they will even go as far as deciding some other person is the decision maker. They decide this because that person appears to be easier to contact and less frustrating to deal with.

The three main steps to chasing down the decision maker are:

1. Correctly identify the decision maker

2. Contact the decision maker

3. Win over the decision maker.

All of these steps must be completed to ensure your success.

Sales Leaders get in early and build a solid relationship with the decision maker. They realize that without a relationship in place between themselves and the decision maker, they will probably lose the sale in the end. Be persistent when you are trying to get in front of the decision maker. What works for me is explain to the decision maker that in order to fairly evaluate all possibilities they need to give you time to explain your offering. There are different ways you can say this but that point needs to be emphasized.

Building a relationship with the decision maker can be difficult if they know your only motive is to win the sale and then you are back on the road never to be seen again. That is why it is so important to build relationships early. Build relationships with key people long before there is ever a sales campaign. When a potential sale appears on the horizon, wouldn't you feel great to know that you already have a solid relationship in place with the decision maker? Sales Leaders know and use this tactic.

GETTING TO KNOW THE DECISION MAKER

All decision makers can decide in your favor. Some of them however, will avoid you at all costs. Usually there is a good reason for this and in most cases it is because they have already aligned themselves with a competitor. This is all the more reason for you to build your relationship with the decision maker early in the game.

Win Tip

Finding the decision maker is critical for your success.

When building a relationship with a decision maker you should learn as much as you can about them. Actually, in order to build a strong relationship, you first need to uncover certain items in their personal life as well as their business world. Get a clear understanding of their goals, intentions, work ethic and position. Make sure you uncover this data before you even start on that relationship.

The decision maker has the same goal as most other people on his or her team. The end result, therefore, is no different. The only subtle change is the process of getting there.

TEAMING WITH
THE DECISION MAKER

Getting on side with the decision maker is only one step in a successful sales campaign. Teaming with the decision maker will ultimately guarantee you the victory. This critical step should not be missed in any sales campaign.

A few years ago I watched a Sales Leader become victorious in three back-to-back sales campaigns with the same customer, generating millions of dollars in business. He generated more success in subsequent years simply because he continued to use the same methodology in all his sales campaigns. Teaming with the decision maker generated an unbelievable amount of success for this one sales person and it can do the same for you.

When you team with the decision maker, you are working toward the same goal with the same process and the same solution. The first step is to understand exactly what the decision maker wants or needs. Can you provide exactly what the decision maker is looking for and do you have the personality to put all of this together in a manner where it becomes a win-win situation for both parties?

When building a relationship with a key decision maker, please remember it must be two-sided. The decision maker needs to understand your goals and you need to understand his. Therefore, a relationship generated with a decision maker must be based on honesty, trust and attaining similar goals.

The best way to team with a decision maker is to understand and address each and every one of their needs. He or she is going to make a decision sometime in the future and should you be able to deliver everything they are asking for, your chances of victory will be greatly improved.

You will need to work three angles while teaming with a decision maker in order to be successful. First, build a strong relationship. Without a strong relationship, parts of your sales campaign may be at risk and you might not be victorious. Building a strong relationship properly with a key decision maker can take you to victory lane.

Next, understand exactly what the decision maker is looking for and give it to him. Decision makers are the same everywhere. They have needs that must be addressed with solutions. Leverage your key relationship to address these needs with your solution.

Finally, utilize your ability to sway the decision makers' thinking or influence in your favor. This angle can only be worked once the other two have been completed. You will need a great relationship in place in order to leverage it in the gray areas of decision making.

Ultimately, the decision maker will make a decision that will generate a victory or create a loss for you. The process of making a decision will not go away. Your job is to make a positive impact throughout the process.

ELRUDE

Jack Coleman has been working on a selling campaign for almost seven months and has managed to find and befriend the decision maker. When Jack first heard about this project he developed and implemented a basic strategy – find the decision maker. It took almost two months before Jack could honestly say he learned the name of the decision maker. He was almost led astray twice in these first two months. Individuals told him they were the decision maker and he had no reason not to believe them at the time.

Upon further evaluation and questioning, Jack realized who the ultimate decision maker really was. He focused more on this individual and eventually met him. The first meeting was awkward but as other meetings were held, the business relationship began to grow.

The sales person and the decision maker realized that not only were they pursuing potential business dealings together, but they had lots in common from a personal perspective as well.

The relationship simply grew stronger and stronger.

With decision time just around the corner, Jack feels that he is in a great position for the win. He also knows that no other sales person has a relationship with the decision maker that is as strong as his.

Elrude 16-1

Elrude Noclue found out about this project three months ago. He made a phone call to the main receptionist in the customers' office and asked who was working on this project. The receptionist gave him a name and a phone number and Elrude was off to the races.

Believing he was talking with the decision maker he dove in at full speed. Never stopping to look back, or in any other direction for that matter, Elrude confidently pushed onward.

Again, with decision time just around the corner, Elrude feels he is in a great position for the win. He doesn't have a clue about what his competition is doing but he is confident that he is finally in control. He even tells his manager he has this one in the bag. Finally, he will get his first win.

A week later the decision is made and the project is awarded to Jack Coleman and his company. Elrude was devastated. He was so sure he had won and when he called his customer to find out what happened; his customer told Elrude he had been overruled. Elrude questioned how he could be overruled when he was the decision maker and his customer told him he wasn't the decision maker.

Throughout the entire campaign Elrude never asked about the decision maker. He assumed his contact was in control of the project. Dejected, Elrude went for a drive in his car to gather his thoughts. How was he going to tell his manager about this and keep his job?

Jack Coleman was ecstatic because he had won again. He also felt sad for Elrude. He had been watching Elrude through the sales campaign and knew that he was heading for trouble again. If only Elrude had someone to spend time with him and teach him the basics of selling. It is a fine line between never winning and being successful. He just needs to do more things right.

Summary

Every sale has a decision maker and you may or may not be able to influence that decision in your favor. Covering your bases with the decision maker will make your job easier, create more victories and take the element of bad surprises out of your sales campaigns.

Never chase a sale without first identifying the decision maker and then compiling a list of tasks you need to accomplish in order to get to the decision maker. A decision maker makes decisions. Should you only have time to cover one person per sale, that person should be the decision-maker. Increase your chances of success by going directly to the source.

Finding the Decision Maker is the toughest part of most sales campaigns. Many decision makers don't identify themselves. On the other hand, influencers want to convince you they are the ultimate decision maker. You will be forced to evaluate all participants to find the true decision maker before you move into the selling process.

Win Process:
Finding the Decision Maker

☑ Power   Ability to create sales success

☑ Partner   The same win-win as you

☑ Teaming   Success for more then one

☑ Honesty   You in a nutshell

☑ Trust   Customers won't buy without it

☑ Communication   Allowing your customer to talk

☑ Decision Maker   The person with the power

☑ Chameleon   A typical decision maker

Win Notes: My Decision Maker

Use this page to assess your ability to find and connect with decision makers. What are your strengths? Where do you need to improve?

17 Presenting

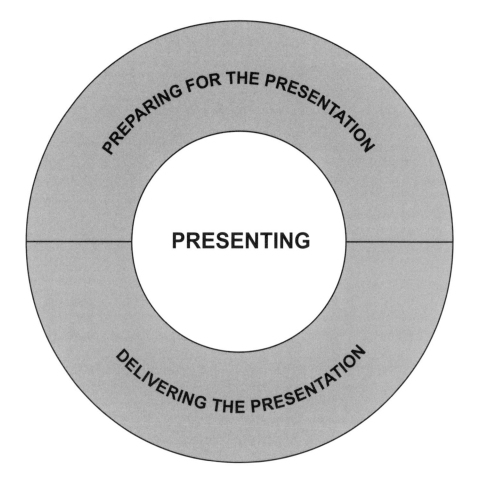

Presenting

17

One of the final pieces of the sales campaign is the presentation. Once you have uncovered the opportunity, gathered all the information, understood the customer needs, and met all the key decision makers, you now have to deliver a flawless presentation. If you don't, all your hard work to this point could be all for naught.

There are two parts to your presentation – preparation and delivery. Although the first part will take much longer to complete than the second portion, each is equally important. Should you prepare well, then your chances of delivering a first rate presentation that can clinch the victory for you, will be much easier. When coupled with a top-of-the-line delivery, you and your value proposition will be hard to beat. Let's take a closer look at how to prepare and present a top-of-the-line presentation that will help you leave your competition in the dust.

PREPARING FOR THE PRESENTATION

Have you ever been given enough time to prepare for a presentation? If you're like most sales people, the answer is no. Being unprepared can certainly take away your control and undermine all the time and effort you have put into your sales campaign to this point. We discussed earlier how important it is to stay in control all the way through your sales campaign. Losing control here by not being prepared is unacceptable. It would be like leading in a car race until the last lap. By giving up the control that late in the game you are surely giving up the victory to your competition.

But how do you prepare when the customer asks to see your presentation immediately? My answer is always the same. Start preparing for your presentation the day you start your sales campaign. You know that sometime during the sales campaign you will be asked to provide a presentation. Why not start now?

Many years ago one of my mentors taught me to prepare for my presentation early in the game. I was taught to always be ready. Although there is a proper time to deliver your presentation, you can actually be asked to present at a time when you least expect it and you may not be ready to deliver with impact. This could eliminate your chance of victory.

Win Tip

Always be prepared to present, and leave your competition in the dust.

So how do you prepare for a presentation that will take place sometime in the future, when today you don't know much of the information needed to help you present?

Earlier in the book we discussed the need to continually qualify the sales opportunity. One of the reasons we do this is so we have the most current information about the need, timeframe, decision making process, etc. We need to know what is happening with the customer every step of the way. If something changes, we need to know that immediately. That way, if you are unexpectedly asked to present your information, you are ready. And believe me, this does happen.

When you are preparing for your upcoming presentation, keep in mind what your customer wants to see. If you were selling a car, your presentation would be the test drive. This is where you get to deliver the goods back to the customer. It will be important for you to gather all the information needed so you can provide the right car for the test drive. When your customer is looking for a truck and you present a small car for the test drive, your presentation has jeopardized your sale.

Don't be reactive about your presentation. It is a valuable part of your sales campaign and should be played out at the right time, for the right person and filled with the right solution.

ELRUDE

Elrude Noclue and Jack Coleman both received calls from the customer within the same hour. They were asked to complete their presentations the next day. They had two hours each.

Jack asked to go first and his wish was granted. He was already prepared except for a few small details. He fine tuned his presentation the night before and was ready for the stage the next morning.

Great presentation!

Elrude 17-1

When Jack started his presentation he stood at the front of the boardroom with his high-tech presentation ready to go. This was the time to show his customer he could provide exactly what the customer wanted to buy. Jack spent the previous eleven months digging and scraping to find all this information, and now it was about to pay off.

He focused on the decision maker but involved each person in the room. He methodically went through each part of his presentation, providing the right answers to the questions the customer asked. His customers were impressed.

Jack was dressed for the event wearing a dark blue suit with a white dress shirt and a matching tie. His shoes were polished and clean. He represented the professional that he really was. He was on his game and the customer could tell.

Jack came to win and he felt quite at home living this life on the stage.

When the presentation was complete he shook everyone's hands and thanked them all. He packed up his equipment and left quickly because he knew other sales people would be presenting next and he wanted them to have time to prepare.

Elrude Noclue arrived several minutes before his presentation time. He looked around the room but did not see an overhead projector. There was a chuckle from the others in the room when he asked if they had such a machine.

Almost ten minutes had passed before someone brought in an old dusty projector. There was another chuckle from the audience as Elrude struggled to get it operational. As he walked toward the nearest electrical plug with cord in hand he managed to pull the entire projector off the table. There was an eruption of laughter as the projector crashed to the floor and was rendered unusable.

Elrude panicked for a moment as he wondered how he was going to show his customers what he would be selling them. He decided that he would just hold up his overheads so they could see them.

Elrude reached into his briefcase and brought out his pile of overheads. He started his presentation by holding up the first overhead as laughter erupted in the room again. Elrude looked at his overhead and it was covered with different colored ink splotches. It took him a moment to realize what had happened.

When Elrude wrote on these blank overheads a couple of hours ago with markers, he didn't realize he needed to let them dry before he put one on top of the other. He flipped through his pile and checked. They were all the same.

Elrude was now lost. He didn't have a clue what to say so he suggested everyone should take a break, even though they had just started. Elrude had to regroup and he wasn't sure how to do that. The problem got worse when the customers decided not to take a break and asked him to continue.

Elrude realized he did not know what his customers wanted. He also realized he never asked them what they wanted and he didn't know what to show them, so he started asking questions.

After thirty-five minutes, one of the customers stood up and asked Elrude to leave. He told Elrude he was only wasting their time and he didn't really know what they wanted anyway.

Elrude 17-2

Elrude argued that he had two hours and told the customer to sit until he was finished. Elrude had decided he was going to take control.

The customer told Elrude to leave before he threw him out. Elrude told the customer he wasn't big enough to throw him out. The customer got up from his chair and walked around the table toward Elrude and stopped about six inches from his face. Elrude swallowed hard as they stared each other down.

After a minute the customer backed away and whacked his hand down on the table as hard as he could, making a loud clap.

Elrude jumped up from his breakfast table in a flash. Where

was he? His friend Slick Nick was standing beside him laughing. Elrude had fallen asleep at his kitchen table late last evening as he was preparing for his presentation. Nick had dropped in because Elrude was not yet in the office and it was now almost ten o'clock in the morning. When Nick whacked his hand on the table Elrude awoke from his dream in an instant.

He missed his presentation. It was scheduled to start now but he was unprepared and an hour away. He called his customer, apologized and conceded defeat.

A week passed before Jack was awarded the victory. His presentation was flawless. Elrude, on the other hand was already off chasing another project. Next time he would be the victor. He is going to execute the wildest, most exciting close anyone will have ever witnessed.

It doesn't matter what you are selling, the steps will always be the same. Present what your customer wants to see and your chances of victory will improve.

You also must know who will be attending your presentation. If you are selling an automobile to a single male or female, then that person will be all that is needed in attendance for the presentation, or in this case, the test-drive.

If you are selling a new house to a couple, then they both will be your audience. If you are selling a financial package to a large business corporation, there may be many people attending your presentation. Find out who will be attending and prepare accordingly.

Win Tip
Know your audience.

I don't think you would feel comfortable finding out at the last minute that someone who gives you grief will be attending your presentation. Find out in advance who the attendees will be and plan accordingly. For example, if you know one of the attendees asks numerous irrelevant questions, mention at the beginning of your presentation that you have a lot of ground to cover and would prefer if everyone held their questions until the end. That way you ensure you will get through your presentation within the allotted time.

Be sure to address this remark directly to the decision maker and get their agreement. This way, all members of your audience know this ground rule will stick.

While preparing for your presentation always have a goal in mind. What do you need to accomplish during this presentation? When you are trying to sell a house to a couple, you should have a goal in mind about results of the house showing or the presentation.

Let's say for example, that the couple entertains year round. You are able to find this out early in your analysis and in your preparation stage you work the idea into the presentation. By showing them how areas in the new house are perfect for entertaining other people, you are giving them something they are looking for. That something and the feeling that goes with it becomes the result you are looking for.

The power of a successful sales campaign is one of the greatest forces a sales person can leverage. This power comes from completing all the small steps along the path to victory. Prepare and present the idea, concept, change or value of a new product or solution. This guideline applies in every industry. Set objectives before the presentation and accomplish them during the presentation.

Win Tip
Great presentations are derived from creativity and planning.

This will bring you to the last preparation point. You can either present first, last or in between. Although I don't know of any one time that is better then the others, I do have my favorite.

I like to be first. My reasons are simple. Whenever I get to present first, at least I get to present. Sometimes, customers will find what they want after the first or second presentation and they will make their decision before they go any further. You may not even get to present if you take your turn at the end and even if you do, your customer has already made their decision no matter what you present.

Another reason why I like to present first is so I can set the standard for all the presentations that will follow. I continually set the bar as high as I can and it becomes very difficult for the sales people who follow me to keep up, especially if they are not prepared.

Preparation is important if you plan on being successful. Lack of preparation by your competition will make you even more successful.

DELIVERING THE PRESENTATION

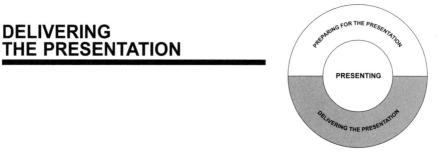

The first item of your presentation should be your agenda. The opportunity for surprises declines greatly if both you and your customer know what the presentation is going to be about. It also serves as a way to ensure you will cover all areas. At the beginning of your presentation, review your agenda with the customer and ask if there is anything else the customer would like to cover. If the answer is yes, you have identified an area of interest to the customer your competition may not know about.

Preparation is wonderful but without an agenda you might forget some important parts of your presentation. Remember, there are many steps and forgetting only one can change a victory into a loss.

Win Tip

You must have some knowledge about what you are selling.

Throughout your presentation, you will be required to use different types of presenting tools. These can range from pictures to proposals. They can also be the item for sale itself like an automobile, a house or a piece of clothing. Larger boardroom presentations can involve equipment like digital projectors, overhead projectors, SMART Boards, cameras, testing equipment, flip charts, whiteboards or handouts.

Use tools that fit and use as many as possible. When used properly these tools will enhance whatever it is you are trying to sell.

When preparing for your presentation, make sure you use all the information you have accumulated through your efforts so far in your sales campaign. Don't be satisfied until you are satisfied. You are now ready for the presentation.

Since you have all the information you need at your fingertips, there will be no excuse for an average presentation. You have worked hard to get to this point in the campaign. It is now time to deliver a presentation with impact.

Summary

Use the tools, use the information, prepare thoroughly, deliver what they want, set your presentation goals and present with confidence. Picture the victory before you start and you will deliver a presentation that will clearly stand out as the best.

Win Tip

A presentation with impact moves you one step closer to victory.

Once you have completed this the first time, set it as your standard. I know its hard work but victories put more money in your pocket then losses. Raise the bar high and keep it there. Distance yourself from your competition.

Your professional image and successful presentation will make your sales life much easier and will play a major part in your future success. Why would you just present when you can present with impact and win?

Presenting your solution is the culmination of all your hard work to this point. Prepare thoroughly and present with confidence.

Win Process:
Presenting

☑ Stage	Where you work
☑ Equipment	Weapons for mass success
☑ Presentation	Your turn to talk
☑ Delivery	The way you present
☑ Going First	The best place
☑ Setting the Bar	As high as you can
☑ Audience	Know in advance who they are
☑ Handouts	Leave them with something

Win Notes: My Presentation

Use this page to assess your presentation skills. What are your strengths? Where do you need to improve?

18

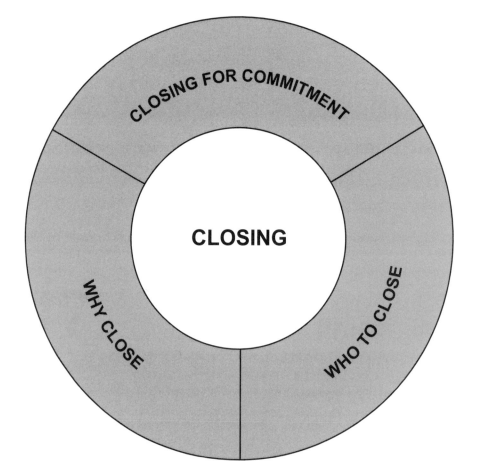

Closing 18

Closing the sale is nothing more then completing one task and moving on to the next. If all the tasks have been completed properly, then the outcome is obvious. Many people think closing is the big surprise that happens at the end of every sales campaign. If you are not in control of your sales campaign, then the win or loss at the end of the campaign may be a big surprise for you. This is not how Sales Leaders perform. While asking for the order is important, it is in fact, a series of small closes along the way that puts you in position to ask for that order.

Closing the sale is about closing for commitment along the way and not closing the entire sales campaign with some magical touch after you failed to gain any commitment along the way. I don't know why we would even think like that.

In this chapter, we will learn how to close at each step of the sales campaign. We will deal with the actual close itself and finish with commitments after each close.

CLOSING FOR COMMITMENT

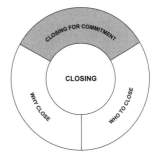

Closing for commitment can be very difficult for sales people. Individual pieces of the sales campaign seem to be relatively easy but when it comes to closing, many sales people fall apart. Let's learn about closing with confidence and putting ourselves in a better position for victory.

The first rule in closing should give you great comfort: It is your right as a sales person to ask for a commitment before moving on to the next step.

Earlier in this book we talked about continually qualifying the opportunity. We do this to ensure we are always on the right track. If something changes, we need to know about it immediately so we can evaluate the new decision criteria and determine if we are still able to provide what is requested by the customer. If not, and we cannot change the decision criteria, we will likely cut our losses early and walk away from this opportunity. There is no point in chasing an opportunity we cannot win.

Closing for commitment at each stage is the same idea. If the customer is no longer interested in our solution, and we cannot change his mind or our deliverable, we need to know that as early as possible in the sales process. If this happens, we need to cut our losses and pursue other opportunities where we have a better fit for what is required by the customer and therefore a better chance at winning. In addition to freeing up your time to pursue another qualified opportunity, your customer will appreciate your honesty as well as the time you have saved him.

Win Tip

Sales Leaders close for commitment along the way.

Some of the events leading up to the sale of an automobile might look like this. The customer enters the vehicle lot for the first time. The sales person is on him in a flash. A question and answer period unfolds and the sales person shows the customer a vehicle. More questions are asked and then the customer wants to test drive in a vehicle he can't afford. Back on the lot a half hour later the sales person asks the customer for his name. Shortly after the customer releases his first name, he leaves the lot, never to return. The sales person returns to his desk to wait for yet another customer. So what just happened here? No commitment from either party for the next step. Chances are the sales person has no idea what the customers' next step will be. Chances are the customers' next step will not involve that sales person.

This practice happens far too often in the automobile dealerships of the world. Actually, it happens far too often whenever sales people are involved.

In a closing for commitment scenario, the automobile sales person would ask some direct questions before any test drive, such as:

- What type of vehicle does the customer want?
- What is the customer's financial position? Can the customer afford the vehicle?
- What color, body style, horsepower, etc. is the customer looking for?
- What other vehicles has the customer looked at?
- When does the customer plan to makes his purchase?
- Does anyone else have a say in the decision, like a spouse?
- What decision criteria will be used to select a vehicle?

The sales person should never let that test drive happen without getting the information from the customer that will show the customer is serious. It will just become a waste of the sales person's time if a test drive is taken without the question period beforehand.

What might happen is, when the sales person is out riding with a potential customer who has no intent of buying, a qualified customer might drop in and another sales person in the company starts working his way to a sale. He wins and the other sales person loses. If this is your approach in selling, you must stop this from happening or you will not be in the business very long.

When you ask a few important questions and your potential customer becomes evasive about answering them and maybe even goes as far as not answering any of them at all then you have to make a decision. Go for joyrides with people or sell vehicles.

Develop some rules and stick to them. Before anybody test drives your product there needs to be some information flowing from customer to sales person. You ask the questions and they give you the answers. Based on these answers you decide if they should go for a test drive or not. Don't let tire-kickers waste your time. You are the only person who should be in control of your success. Whatever happens is because of you and no one else. We all know that each sale is different but you should develop procedures and use common sense to put them into action.

I know if I were selling vehicles, I would not take anyone for a test drive unless I knew I had a chance of making a sale. You should follow the same guideline.

Also, try not to let the test drive close the sale for you. Always be closing for some kind of commitment to move you a step closer to victory.

ELRUDE

Jack Coleman had been chasing a potential sale for a couple of months and has been closing for commitment along the way. He summarized each meeting to ensure he clearly understood the customers' criteria and where Jack, his product and his company stood in the mind of the decision maker. Jack ensured all criteria and concerns were addressed to the satisfaction of the customer before he moved on to the next step. The customer felt comfortable with Jack's approach.

Jack gave his customer exactly what he was looking for at a price the customer was willing to pay. Most of all, the customer felt at ease dealing with Jack. He was approachable, pleasant, knowledgeable and creative.

When decision time arrived the project was awarded to Jack. He distanced himself so far ahead of his competition it wasn't even close.

Jack Coleman won this project for many reasons. Among them was his ability to close for commitment all through the different steps of the selling campaign. He managed to get his customer to agree with each and every step before moving on to the next.

Customers are sometimes afraid to make that big decision at the end of the selling campaign. Jack's process is to have the customer make many small decisions along the way. When the selling campaign comes to an end, there is no large decision to be made by the customer, only a small one – to make the award.

Elrude Noclue worked hard on this project. He asked many questions and continually verified his assumptions. He plodded through the selling campaign for two months and he was convinced he knew exactly what his customer wanted.

Unfortunately when it came time for the big close, Elrude was turned down flat. The last time he felt this way was in tenth grade when he asked Betty to go on a date. In front of all his friends, she told him, under no certain terms, no!

A week later Elrude called his customer and asked him where he went wrong. His customer told him that although he liked his close, his timing was three days too late, his price was twenty percent too high and he didn't want all the features Elrude was trying to sell him.

Do you know anything about selling???

I just don't get it. Why do I lose all the time?

Elrude 17-1

The customer told Elrude the sales person who won the order validated throughout the selling process what the customer wanted and when the end of the selling campaign arrived, the decision was easy.

Closing for commitment is actually a simple procedure. Whenever your customer agrees with a feature and you can get them to nod or say yes, I like or want that, you are closing for commitment. Each time you do this, you are moving closer to the victory. The more nods you get, the better your chances.

When your customer is buying something from you it must be competitively priced. Early in the sales campaign, find out if your standard price is competitive. If not, you need to reconsider your position and adjust your price, look for superior differentiation in your product, or cut your losses and discontinue the sales campaign. Customers also buy size, color, shape, sound, aroma and more. Your job is to convince your customer to accept the feature with an acknowledgement. Obtain many small acknowledgements throughout the sales campaign and you are continually moving closer to victory.

Win Tip
When there is no validation, usually there is no commitment.

Many sales people present all the features and benefits but are not successful in gaining the customers' acknowledgement of these features and benefits. There is no validation when this takes place, therefore there is no commitment. Don't wait until the end of the sales campaign to find out this is happening.

WHO TO CLOSE

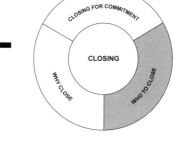

I have watched sales people try to close for commitment throughout a sales campaign and in the end they lost because they were not dealing with the decision maker. This is not only a depressing situation to put yourself into but it is a serious waste of your time. Many of my sales victories involved my competition trying to close someone who was not the decision maker.

The quantity of competitors in today's market has grown tremendously, but the quantity of Sales Leaders has not followed the same trend. As long as you can stay in the game, you will increase your chances of winning. The profession of selling has become watered down over the last decade or two. It presents a perfect scenario for you to learn all about the game and go out there and become a Sales Leader.

One of the most important lessons to learn in sales is finding the decision maker. You can't sell a vehicle to me when the only person you have been talking with and showing vehicles to is my spouse. I am making the final decision; therefore I am the one you need to be discussing the sale with. I have found, on numerous occasions that sales people I have competed against were in fact selling to people who were not decision makers. This makes my job quite a bit easier and of course their job becomes much harder.

Win Tip

Always close the decision maker.

Large business-to-business sales campaigns usually have many people involved in the decision making process. We talked earlier in this book about how to get to the decision maker and now we have to learn from that information and work hard at closing for commitment. We should be closing for commitment with the right people – the decision makers. They are the only ones who can make the decisions you need them to make to guarantee both your success and their satisfaction. Gain your closing commitment from these decision makers and you will be rewarded more often.

WHY CLOSE

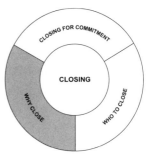

Simply put, if I do not close, I will not win. This is a given in the sales profession. Closing for commitment along the way sets up a successful journey in your sales campaigns. There are three different paths that can be taken by each and every sales person when it comes to chasing a sale. The first path is not to close at all. The second path is to incorrectly close and the third path is to close properly. Let's discuss these distinct paths so you can decide what to do and what not to do in your sales campaigns to guarantee the success you deserve.

The first path, not closing at all, will guarantee you failure and job loss and set you up for a life of financial and emotional hardship. Not closing a sale is like losing in the last inning of a baseball game while standing up at the plate and never swinging the bat. It compares to giving up. I am sure this is not done intentionally, however, for those who don't know how to get away from this scenario it becomes extremely difficult to compete in any sales campaign.

Once we move from one step in the sales campaign to the next we must successfully close for commitment to move forward. We do not want to put ourselves into a position where we have completed some steps in our campaign only to find we didn't effectively close on one of the previous steps. Let me show you an example that I saw a sales team get themselves involved with that ended in defeat for them.

Two large companies formed a partnership to chase business in one industry sector. The sales team started chasing a variety of projects. One of these projects offered a unique challenge for the team. The project was large in comparison to some of the others they were working on, however the project type did not differ very much from the norm.

The customer threw up a flag early in the sales campaign about this sales company's ability to execute on previous projects. From a customer's point of view there was concern that even though both companies in the partnership have proven experience, they had not yet completed any projects together. The customer's project was large enough the decision maker felt he should go with a proven company. He could not justify taking the risk with a newly formed partnership.

This is where the problem occurred. The sales person in charge of the campaign knew all about this issue but continued to ignore it hoping it would go away. Many weeks passed and a number of other steps in the campaign were completed but that issue was still there. The sales person told no one in his company about the ongoing issue. When there were only a few days left before the decision was to be made, the sales person told his manager about the issue that would probably keep him from winning the project. The manager was obviously upset – the sales person knew about the issue for many weeks but chose to ignore it.

The manager suggested the issue could probably be dealt with but not in the few days that were left. There was a last minute attempt by both manager and sales person but the decision was made and the competition was awarded the work. The project was worth millions of dollars.

The sales person's company spent thousands of dollars flying people from country to country trying to win this work but by missing one step in the closing cycle, all was lost. The sales person did not close for commitment along the way. He missed only one step but it was enough to cost him the victory.

Another common way in which sales people get themselves into trouble is constantly providing information to their customer and getting nothing in return. When the decision is made and the sales person loses the deal, quite often they have no real idea why the deal was lost. The customer usually offers a vague reason and the sales person is left scratching his head. Better luck next time I guess. You must be in control of the sales campaign in order to claim the victory. When you don't close, you are taking yourself out of this control position and setting up your demise.

Closing incorrectly can be almost as hazardous as not closing at all. Sometimes victories may be generated but usually the success level is quite limited. Many things can go wrong when you are closing incorrectly. You may be closing the wrong person, closing at the wrong time, closing for the wrong reason or closing the wrong concept. All the while, your competition is closing properly, putting them in a better position for victory.

The best way to close correctly is to deal with facts only. Do not assume anything in the sales campaign. Once you start to assume details and work your closing tasks around those ideas, you could be right or you could be wrong. You should not take chances like that. Set a goal that you are going to win and get the facts so you can close properly.

This now brings us to the proper way to close. We have learned over the years about a variety of closing techniques. We can use the aggressive close, the assumptive close, the sympathy close, the price close, the deadline close, the relationship close, the competitive close, the quality close and a dozen others. Although these all have their place in various sales campaigns, I believe they are all based on the big close at the end of the process. I also believe this is not the way a sales campaign should end. We need to be closing for commitment throughout the sales campaigns and not waiting for the grand finale to drape a customer with some fancy closing technique.

Win Tip
Never be satisfied until you are satisfied.

Summary

Many cases have proven if you close for commitment along the way, you may never need to ask for the order at all. The customer will just give it to you at the end. Within the final few steps of the sales campaign both customer and sales person realize there is only one solution. The order is placed and the sales person moves on to the next campaign to start the process all over again.

Closing a sale is a fulfilling event. It means you won. It means that you came first. Two things are for sure; if you are good at closing, you will win more often but if you are not very good at closing, you will lose many times. Always be closing for commitment throughout your entire sales campaign.

Win Process:
Closing

☑ Order	Ask for it
☑ Validation	Agreement
☑ Victory	Your continued goal
☑ Please	Used when asking for the order
☑ Along the Way	When to close
☑ Decision Criteria	Understand it
☑ Who do I close	The decision maker
☑ Successful Closer	A Sales Leader

Win Notes: My Closing

Use this page to assess your closing skills. What are your strengths?
Where do you need to improve?

Section 3: Winning the Game

Summary

Becoming a Sales Leader is all about winning. You are hired to win, not just compete. And now you are ready to prove yourself.

Selling campaigns begin with prospecting. Know your territory. Know your competition.

Once you have developed your prospect list, spend time creating opportunities and positioning your company for the victories that lie ahead. Create value by finding solutions to problems your customers don't even know exist.

Fully understand the role of the decision maker. Getting to know them and their decision making criteria will place you in the best possible winning position at all times.

Preparing and delivering your presentation with impact will move you ahead of your competition. Know what your customer is looking for and wants to hear. The presentation should not contain any surprises.

We are now at the end of the game. If you have been closing for commitment throughout your campaign, the victory should be yours.

Sales Leaders win the game because they play to win.

A note from Ron,

I certainly hope you take many new ideas from this book and implement them into your selling campaigns with greater success being the result. Maybe some of the ideas are not new, but in fact, rejuvenated from your memories and maybe used in previous successes. Whatever the case, I hope you enjoyed my book.

My idea from the start has been to publish a book full of useful knowledge for sales people in almost any industry. Equally as important is the design of the content of this book. I have tried to keep it lighthearted by using Jack and Elrude to drive home some of my points.

I truly believe there is a little bit of Jack in all of us and unfortunately there is a little bit of Elrude in all of us as well. Both of these characters will be back in my next book proving yet again there is a winner and a loser.

Six years ago I started working on my dream and here we are today with book in hand. Please use the data in this book as a reference to greater success. I encourage you to keep notes as you read through it for the first time and refer back to it when you need pieces of information that will help you win. After all, winning is the reason why we are in this wonderful world called sales.

Have fun winning,
Ron MacKinnon

A note from Jack,

I had fun winning my way through this book. I feel that if I am going to do something, I may as well do it right. As a child, I was taught never to waste anything. I apply this learning to all my sales efforts.

Working on a potential sale which I am going to lose is a waste of my valuable time. Most of my competition will spend days and weeks working on a project they know they are not going to win. I don't see any logic in that.

I hope my exploits throughout this book have helped you in some way. If you take only one new idea and apply it successfully, then this book will have been worthwhile.

You can be as successful as me. You just have to do what I do. I don't like to lose so usually I don't. Use the Win Process to your advantage and leave your competition behind. Develop a desire to succeed and you will be more successful then you ever dreamed possible.

Regards,
Jack Coleman

A note from Elrude,

I hope you enjoyed my exploits as I tried to win my first sale. It frustrates me a great deal to put in the effort I do and have nothing to show for it. I guess I have realized that I must make many changes if I am going to succeed in the sales profession.

I hope you have learned from my mistakes and don't do what I have been doing. There are too many sales people out there just like me and we all tend to lose more then we should. People like Jack have no problem defeating people like us.

I will be back in the next book still looking for that first victory. I am not giving up. I know I will be successful one day, more then I ever dreamed possible.

Stay pumped,
Elrude Noclue

Coming soon from Canadian Bestselling author –
Ron MacKinnon

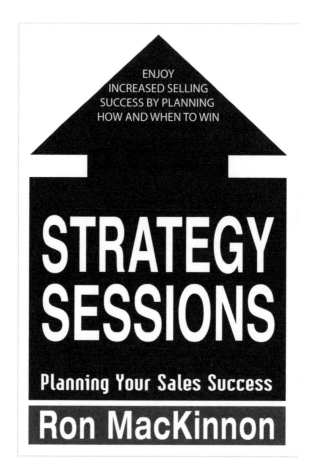

Soon to be released, *Strategy Sessions* will take an in-depth look at how a Sales Leader operates from day to day. You will see how real strategies are used to gain control of sales campaigns and generate successful endings. You will see how strategy and planning will help you exceed all your quota's and you will see how a long term strategy will help position you to having better accounts, promotions, improve your closing ratio and offer greater wealth. For more information on this book check out Montgomery Harrison Corporation at www.thewinprocess.com.

MONTGOMERY HARRISON CORPORATION

Montgomery Harrison Corporation is a sales and marketing company with specifics in Publishing, Sales Training, Coaching and a distribution arm for sales material.

For more information on the company and our products and service, please contact us at - www.thewinprocess.com

Vote on-line for your favorite *Elrude*

Montgomery Harrison Corporation
Contact: Ron MacKinnon, President & Author
Phone: 403-819-6288
Email: ron@thewinprocess.com

Here's another great book for your library…

THE POWER OF FOCUS
HOW TO HIT YOUR BUSINESS, PERSONAL AND FINANCIAL TARGETS WITH ABSOLUTE CERTAINTY
Jack Canfield, Mark Victor Hansen and Les Hewitt

'If you only read one book this millennium… *The Power of Focus* should be it!"
Harvey Mackay
Author, Swim with the Sharks

"Great book!
An amazingly simple plan that will benefit everyone who implements it."
Stephen Covey
Author, The 7 Habits of Highly Effective People

Available in Bookstores
For Volume discounts
Toll Free 877-678-0234

ACCELERATE YOUR PROGRESS WITH EXPERT COACHING!

THE POWER OF FOCUS

THE ACHIEVERS COACHING PROGRAM consists of small groups of qualified business people who are keen to jump to an even higher level of performance and income. Each group meets every two months for a whole day under the leadership of an experienced **ACHIEVERS COACH**.

The purpose of this regular time-out is to rethink, refocus, and review your progress as well as brainstorm with other participants. We'll also show you how to create "Big Picture" action plans that will triple your income and double your time off. In addition, you'll learn how to eliminate procrastination, time pressures and unnecessary stress.

> Call today for your FREE copy of THE ACHIEVERS SCORECARD
> --an eye-opening sixteen point checklist that
> will clearly identify your strengths and weaknesses.
>
> **Toll Free 877-678-0234**

PHONE: 403-295-0500   FAX: 403-730-4548   EMAIL: info@achievers.com
WEBSITE : www.achievers.com

SALES SUCCESS:
your reward for being
prepared, persistent and passionate.

Tim Breithaupt, President of Spectrum Training Solutions and author of **Canadian Bestseller**, *Take This Job and Love It: The Joys of Professional Selling*, believes that people can do the most amazing things when stimulated and armed with the right sales tools. He delivers these tools in his book and at his seminars by using a lively blend of sales logic, simplicity and humour. The book's potent combination of essential attitudes and selling skills will help you achieve new levels of success.

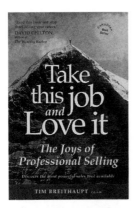

"Tim's insights deliver a surprisingly simple approach to selling. It's a must read – one that I have recommended to all my sales managers."

John Meissner,
Vice President Sales, Fairmont Hotels

Workshops and Keynotes Available

Spectrum Training Solutions designs training programs that deliver the necessary tools and techniques to foster confidence for both professional and personal development. Tim would be flattered to speak at your next sales convention or develop a customized in-house training program.

* Sales Training
* Customer Service Skills
* Telephone Skills

* Management Skills
* Negotiation Skills

Building Confidence
Building Sales

SPECTRUM
TRAINING SOLUTIONS

(800) 404-0666
www.spectrain.com

Book design, layout and illustrations by

integration marketing works

www.imworks.biz

Additional Notes:

Additional Notes:

Additional Notes:

Additional Notes:

Additional Notes:

Additional Notes:

Additional Notes:

Additional Notes:

Additional Notes:

Additional Notes: